Jack O'Connor's

GUN BOOK

by Jack O'Connor

Wolfe Publishing Company
6471 Airpark Drive
Prescott, Arizona 86301
1992

Originally Published 1953 by Popular Science Publishing Co., Inc.

Reprinted May 1992

ISBN 1-879356-11-2

WOLFE PUBLISHING COMPANY
6471 Airpark Drive
Prescott, Arizona 86301

Contents

BOOK 1 - Jack O'Connor's Gun Book

BOOK 2 - Handbook for Hunters

Cover Photo

This original First Model Newton rifle is chambered for the classic .30 Newton cartridge -- the first real .30 magnum round. The scope is a Lyman Alaskan in Redfield rings with a specially modified Redfield one-piece base. The gun also has Newton's extra cost cocking piece sight and cheekpiece stock. Obtained in "very used" condition, the rifle was restored by John Campbell and rust blued by gunsmith Charles Danner of Fayetteville, Tenn.

(Photo by Dave Dennison of Dennison Photographic)

JACK O'CONNOR'S
GUN BOOK

BOOK 1

Wolfe Publishing Company
6471 Airpark Drive
Prescott, Arizona 86301

CHAPTER I

What Is Killing Power?

Here's what happens when bullet hits
flesh and why some kill cleaner
than others

K ILLING power is one of the hottest of subjects among riflemen. Get a dozen big-game hunters together, lure them into discussing it, and you'll probably wind up with a dozen different opinions. One man pins his faith to heavy bullets of large diameter. Another likes relatively light bullets at high velocity. A third tells you that placement of shots is so important all else can be disregarded. One says bullet energy is a good indicator of killing power, but the man across the table retorts that energy figures are worthless. A hunter of considerable experience asserts he can handle any North American big game with a .30/06, while the next man rates the .30/06 as only fair on deer and almost worthless on elk and other large game.

The trouble with most evidence on killing power is that it is given by human beings — and many of us are poor observers, have limited experience, and are prejudiced. Killing power varies according to circumstances, hence it does not pay to jump at conclusions. One animal may be harder to kill than another of the same size and species. A frightened animal, it is generally believed, is more difficult to kill than one taken unawares. The heart may be struck when it is full or empty. An animal may be 25 yd. away or 400.

Often results defy analysis. A bull mountain caribou is only slightly smaller than the average bull elk; the first one I ever shot was trotting along an open hillside about 200 yd. away. I was in a good sitting position with a tight sling on my arm. At the first hit with a .270 Silvertip, the bull stopped and stood still on rubbery legs. I put three more 130-gr. bullets through his lungs before he went down. All four were in a group you could cover with the palm of your hand. All went right through the lungs and all were rolled up into little balls under the hide on the far side. The lungs were in shreds and the chest cavity was full of blood. Placement of the shots had been perfect. Bullet action was perfect.

Now, from that one experience, I might have felt justified in concluding that the .270 doesn't have what it takes for a big bull caribou. About a week later I shot another big bull with the same rifle, the same load, the same placement. The only difference was that the second bull was farther away —about 300 yd. He dropped stone dead in his tracks.

In other hunts, I have shot about a dozen bulls with the 130-gr. bullet in the .270 and every one of them has been a one-shot kill.

So conclusion jumping does not pay. Sometimes an animal that's almost shot to pieces will remain on its feet. Other times a relatively superficial wound will knock the same sort of animal cold. Once I shot a big buck mule deer on the run at something over 200 yd. and it fell like a bag of potatoes. I walked over to where it lay and the buck got up and wobbled off. I shot it through the chest, and when I reached it I was astonished to find that the first 150-gr. Remington Bronze Point .30/06 bullet had merely bored a hole through the joint of his right front leg. Why did he go down? Had some mysterious force so shocked his whole system that he collapsed — or had the bullet caught him with most of his weight on his right front leg so that he fell and got his wind knocked out?

Another time I was jackrabbit hunting and shot at a running jack. Down it went. When I reached it I found one front foot shot off and no other wound. What killed it? On another occasion I shot at a bighorn ram just as it was about to top a ridge at close range, somewhere between 50 and 75 yd. I saw one side of the ram's rump change from dingy white to crimson — and then he was over the ridge. I found him stone dead a couple of hundred feet away in the next canyon. Yet the 139-gr. Western 7 mm. bullet had blown up in the rump like a bomb and had not penetrated the body cavity at all. How does one explain the quick death of all these animals?

In September, 1950, a friend of mine in Wyoming shot a big buck antelope running at about 225 yd. The 130-gr. .270 bullet struck the animal across the fleshy part of the rump — a long, long way from any vital area — but that buck died instantly in midair and before six witnesses. What killed him?

The killing power of a bullet is ordinarily determined by two factors

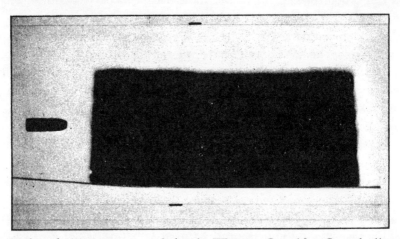

In these ballistics tests, made by the Western Cartridge Co., a bullet is fired into a block of gelatin which has much the same consistency as animal flesh.

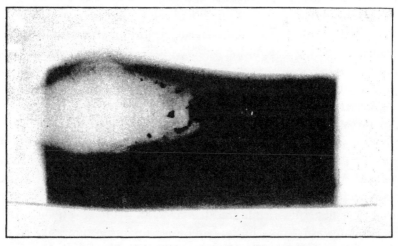

X-Ray shows bullet half way through, mushrooming and shredding metal. Note the "Flash" cavity forming in the block.

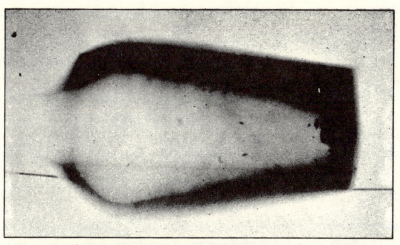

When the bullet emerges and the block returns to normal shape, the big cavity will shrink into a smaller permanent one.

— where it hits and how large an *interior* wound it makes. Even the most unsophisticated know that a shot through the brain, or one that breaks the spine forward of the shoulders, means instant death. It takes no physiologist to know that a broken back anywhere means paralyzed hindquarters and a disabled animal, that a heart shot means quick and sometimes instant death, and that the destruction of much lung tissue also means quick death.

I don't believe that there can be much argument when I say that the larger the wound area in proportion to the size of the animal the quicker the death — or that if the wound area is large enough it will kill an animal, no matter where the bullet hits. The abdominal area back of the diaphragm is nonvital tissue in the sense that it is not *immediately* necessary for life. Naturally, if the whole hind end of an animal is blown off, be it mouse or moose, the animal will quickly die.

The vulnerability of animals obviously varies with their size. Put another way, a wound area that would cover half a woodchuck would cover a much smaller proportion of a coyote, still less of a deer, etc. All else being equal, then, an antelope or a small white-tail deer is easier to kill than a mule deer, a black bear is easier to kill than a grizzly, and an elk or a caribou is easier to kill than a moose. Let us suppose that a certain bullet traveling at a certain velocity will destroy a pound of tissue. That would be 1/100 of the dressed weight of an

9

antelope or small white-tail deer; only 1/500 of a grizzly, caribou, or elk; and only 1/1000 part of a moose or of a large Alaska brown bear.

Most of my hunting has been done with the 130-gr. bullet in the .270 and the 150-gr. bullet in the .30/06. With either, and a chest-cavity hit at a range up to about 250 yd., I have almost always got instant kills on coyotes, antelope, white-tails, mule deer, and sheep. On elk and caribou I have got instant kills something over half the time. I have *never* got a one-shot kill on a moose with either cartridge, and only once have I got one on a grizzly.

My own experience would tend to indicate, then, that the good rifleman shooting a .270 or a .30/06 and placing his shots in the lung area can expect very quick kills on animals that weigh up to about 500 lb. on the hoof; but with a heavier animal he cannot expect instant kills with shots in the lung-heart area.

So it begins to look as if the boys who want a bullet that kills quickly but doesn't destroy meat are reaching for the moon, since killing power and destruction of tissue go hand in hand. The thing to do is to confine the tissue destruction to nonedible areas in the animal — for instance, the lungs.

What is it that gives a bullet power to destroy tissue? The weight, the caliber, the sectional density (which is the relationship of total weight to diameter), the impact velocity, and the construction. Other things being equal, a 300-gr. bullet is a better killer than one weighing 100 gr.; a bullet of .35 caliber is better than one of .25 caliber; a long bullet (one of great sectional density) better than a short one; and a fast bullet better than a slow one.

The large-caliber bullet kills better because it displaces more tissue, just as a dagger displaces more tissue than a needle. A heavier bullet will strike a harder blow, just as a baseball can conk you harder than a tennis ball. The long bullet (all else being equal) will penetrate more deeply and make a correspondingly larger wound than will the short one.

However, bullet *construction* modifies these principles. A light, relatively short bullet can be so strongly constructed that it will penetrate more deeply than a longer, heavier, but weaker and softer bullet. And a small-caliber bullet can be so constructed that it will open up to a large caliber, even in the fragile bodies of crows and woodchucks. On

10

the other hand some bullets, with heavy, full jackets, won't expand at all but drive through the thick hide and heavy bone of rhinos and elephants.

The bullet constructed to drive clear through a rhino and break massive leg bones on the far side isn't worth much as a deer bullet, and one made to explode inside a woodchuck is poor medicine for moose. That's obvious. But to some shooters it is not so obvious that a bullet which will drive through an elk's rump up into his paunch and on into his lungs is a very poor killer on the same animal with a broadside lung shot.

The function of the bullet is to get *inside* an animal and then to shed its energy on the animal's vital tissues, wrecking them. Theoretically, the ideal bullet would remain within the animal, expending all its energy. But I prefer a bullet that will go on through the animal on a broadside shot. It will waste some energy on the landscape in such cases, but it will have enough penetrating power to get into the vitals when you have to shoot at an angle, or break a heavy bone.

In the days of black powder and lead bullets, the only way to increase killing power was to enlarge caliber and bullet weight. Hunters of the largest game used tremendous 4, 6, 8, and 10 bore *rifles*, and many unsophisticated hunters still rate the killing power of a rifle by the size of the hole in the end of the barrel. But since the advent of smokeless powder, killing power has been stepped up (1) by increasing the sectional density of bullets, and (2) by controlling penetration and expansion by jacket thickness, jacket hardness, hardness of core, or various mechanical devices.

It is possible to make a game bullet that will blow up like a bomb, one that will penetrate deeply; one that will maintain its original caliber; and another that will expand to double or triple that caliber. But of all the methods of increasing killing power, the stepping up of velocity has been the most effective. If the bullet is designed to get into the vitals, velocity is the most important factor in killing power. This is the opinion of a pretty high proportion of big-game hunters, of noted ballisticians, and of surgeons who have studied battle wounds.

For many years there has been a running fight (with a lot of noise and few casualties) between advocates of the heavy, large-caliber bullet at moderate velocity and proponents of a lighter bullet of smaller caliber at high velocity. Some of the heavy-bullet boys have gone so

11

far as to say that no modern high-velocity cartridge has as much actual killing power as the old black-powder cartridges like the .45/70 — a statement which to me is absolutely ridiculous.

One question often posed is: "Why does no modern cartridge have the killing power of the .50/110 and why is it that no cartridge can kill game at 1,200 yd. as the buffalo hunters habitually killed buffaloes?"

The answer, of course, is (a) there are a lot of modern cartridges with more killing power than the .50/110, and (b) buffalo hunters didn't kill buffaloes at 1,200 yd.

Greater velocity in a bullet means greater energy, and greater energy means greater destructive power. The cavity in the block at left was caused by a 100-gr. .257 bullet traveling at a muzzle velocity of 1,900 foot seconds, while the cavity in the block at right was caused by the same bullet at a velocity of 2,900 foot seconds.

For a long time the big-bullet boys have been sniping at published figures of bullet energy. Such figures are valueless, they say. Instead they have invented their own terms. One such, has invented the term "pounds feet." Another uses mysterious killing power units based on heaven only knows what, and rates cartridges accordingly.

Actually, extensive tests made at Princeton University during the last war show that the relationship between energy and wound severity is very close. They also show that the often-noted "shock effect" of impact from bullets traveling much faster than 2,000 foot seconds results from sharp *energy* increase as velocities go beyond 2,000.

12

When the .270 with its 130-gr. bullet at 3,140 foot seconds came out, the conservatives looked down their noses at it because of its light bullet. Yet at 200 yd. it delivers 1,850 foot pounds of energy — almost exactly that delivered by the .30/06's 180-gr. bullet fired at a muzzle velocity of 2,720. Experience has proved that it kills just as well as the .30/06 and often better, because on light, thin-shelled game the .270 bullet is likely to shed all or most of its energy within the animal, whereas the heavier .30/06 bullet is likely to go on through and shed only part of its energy.

Let's take a look at what velocity does to energy. A 100-gr. bullet driven at 2,000 foot seconds (roughly the power of the .25/35) turns up 887 foot pounds of energy. Step it up to 3,000 foot seconds (about like the .257) and it delivers 1,996 foot pounds. Give it 4,000 foot seconds and it attains 3,553 foot pounds, or more power than the 180-gr. .300 Magnum cartridge. Step it up to 5,000 foot seconds and the energy more than doubles. Our little 100-gr. bullet is now striking as hard a blow as the very heaviest bullets from double-barreled elephant rifles.

It's true that light, high-speed bullets all too often do not penetrate well enough to deliver their energy in the middle of the animal. Misconstruing that fact, the heavy-bullet boys consider bullet weight a virtue in itself rather than as a means of getting energy to a spot where it does some good.

I once autopsied the carcass of a 600-lb. grizzly shot with a 41-gr. bullet fired from a .22/.250 at about 4,200 foot seconds. First bullet blew up on the shoulder blade and made a superficial wound. (Conclusion: the .22/.250 is no good on large game.) The second bullet slipped between two ribs and killed the bear instantly. (Conclusion: the .22/.250 is a deadly grizzly cartridge.) Two findings, so take your pick.

High-speed photographs showing bullets striking gelatin and other stand-ins for tissue tell us a lot about wounding effect we had to guess at before. For instance, few of us would have dreamed of the enormous "flash" cavities opened up in tissue by high-speed bullets, even though we've seen chucks and jacks literally explode when hit. These temporary cavities are much greater than the permanent ones we find when we dress out game.

Too many of us have judged the severity of the wound simply by

13

the size of the permanent cavity. Some of us have judged it by the size of the bullet's exit hole. We have neglected the killing effect of the bloodshot tissue *around* the permanent wound channel, and the effect of the opening of the temporary cavity.

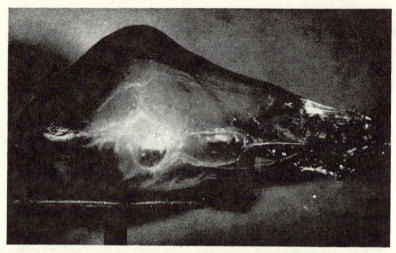

Gelatin blocks in these two photographs were originally the same size. The block above is shown momentarily distorted as a .257 Silvertip bullet passes through it at 2,900 foot seconds. Below the same type of bullet moving at 1,900 foot seconds (as it would at about 300 yards) strikes a block. The distortion is less marked. Similar distortion is caused by a bullet penetrating animal flesh.

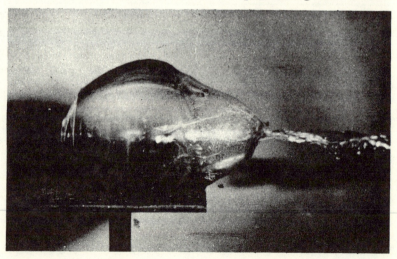

Once the bullet gets inside the animal, the faster it loses its energy, apparently the quicker it kills. That is why observant hunters have noticed that on some animals and in some calibers the new controlled-expanding bullets kill less quickly than old-fashioned, thin-jacketed soft-points with pure lead cores.

In 1951 I shot twice at a very large Dall ram with a certain make of 150-gr. bullet in the .30/06. Both shots were in the rump as he ran away. The first was deflected a bit and came out through the ribs. The second went through from stern to stem and came out the front of the chest. The guide said he saw the ram hump up at the first shot, but I couldn't tell it was hit. Even after the second shot it ran twenty feet or so before it went down. The bullets hadn't shed their energy fast enough.

Exactly the opposite effect was obtained when I hunted deer with the pre-war 120-gr. .270 bullet made by Fred Barnes. It had a thin jacket and soft lead core, and when I sent it off at about 3,250 foot seconds with 52 gr. of No. 4064 powder it blew up like a bomb as soon as it got inside an animal. Every deer I shot with that load was blasted down like a paper doll in a sudden gust of wind.

One grizzly I shot with the .30/06 took four 180-gr. bullets high through the lungs before he fell for keeps. Bullets opened up only slightly, went on through, and I could see all of them crack into rocks or kick up sand on the far side. Another grizzly was killed with the 180-gr. Remington Bronze Point driven at about 3,250 in a .300 Weatherby Magnum. The bullet opened up *fast* and blew a saucer-size hole on the far side. Instant kill!

As the high-velocity missile strikes the animal and opens up, it apparently creates shock waves throughout the body. The larger the bullet and the faster it travels the more violent the waves and the larger the cavity in the bullet's wake, just as the larger the stone and the faster it is hurled, the bigger the waves and the more violent the splash in water.

It is probable that these violent waves, traveling through moisture-filled flesh, often causes quick death even with rather poorly placed shots. A surgeon who is a gun nut and hunter tells me he thinks such quick kills come from injury to the spinal cord by the shock waves. The explanation sounds logical, since the spinal cord is the most delicate part of a mammal's anatomy. Injury so slight that it's hard for a skilled autopsy surgeon to find can kill like lightning, my surgeon friend says.

The faster a bullet is moving, then, the more damage it causes when it strikes. The difference in killing power between the .22 Long Rifle bullet, which gets to the 100-yd. mark traveling at 1,045 foot seconds, and the .220 Swift bullet, zipping along at 3,490, lies largely in the difference in impact velocity. The .22 Long Rifle bullet weighs 40 gr. and the Swift bullet only 8 gr. more. Out at extreme range, when the velocity of the Swift bullet has dropped to that of the .22 rimfire at 100 yd., the Swift has in effect become a .22 Long Rifle.

Over the years, evolution of big-game cartridges has been constantly in the direction of higher velocity. Rifles of the .30/30 class with muzzle velocities of around 2,000 foot seconds were a great improvement over the black-powder cartridges with 1,300-1,500. They were easier to hit with because of flatter trajectory. For the same amount of energy they had less recoil. Grain for grain of bullet weight, they killed better. A jump in velocity of another 1,000 foot seconds in cartridges like the .270 with the 130-gr. bullet and the .30/06 with the 150-gr. bullet was an equally great gain.

And although the .220 Swift is primarily a varmint cartridge, it has shown the way to an entirely new class of big-game cartridges — those with muzzle velocities of 3,500-4,000. Friends of mine who have hunted in Africa with the .257 Weatherby Magnum, which drives an 87-gr. bullet at around 4,000, tell me it kills zebras, which are as large as small horses, as easily as the Swift kills a jackrabbit.

Someday we may be hunting moose and Alaska brown bear with 50-gr. bullets driven at 10,000 foot seconds!

CHAPTER II

How Good Is the .30/06?

Once the undisputed leader of the big
American cartridges, the .30/06 is
now a subject of argument

NOT so many years ago the .30/06 was the undisputed leader of
the more-powerful American calibers. It was the top all-round
big-game cartridge; the No. 1 long-range target load; and it was even
touted as a varmint cartridge by some of its more enthusiastic admirers. That was quite a reputation for a load that started out, in 1906,
as the official U. S. military cartridge.

Then it began to slip a bit in popularity. Even prior to the last war,
the big .300 H.&H. Magnum had surpassed the .30/06 as a long-
range target cartridge. And with the advent of hot 22's like the Hornet, Swift, and the many good wildcats, the .30/06 — with its husky
report and recoil and heavy bullets — is just about out for varmints.
Since the end of the second World War it has had, in the .270, a real
rival as an all-round big-game cartridge.

Now there's some sniping at the .30/06 in the field where it genuinely shines — as an all-round big-game cartridge. It isn't, I've read,
much of a load for the larger American game like elk, caribou, moose,
and grizzly bear, and 'tis said that to tackle an Alaska brown bear with
one would be a reckless act. Not too long ago I saw a list of cartridges
suitable for elk. The .30/06 was not on it but the ancient .45/70 was,
as was the 8x57 mm. Mauser with the 236-gr. bullet.

I may be a dope, but after many sleepless nights of brooding I'll be
dog-goned if I can see where an 8 mm. Mauser with a 236-gr. bullet

has anything on a .30/06 with a 220-gr. bullet except a slightly larger hole in the barrel. Prior to the war, the 236-gr. 8 mm. Mauser was loaded to a muzzle velocity of 2,100 foot seconds and muzzle energy of 2,230 foot pounds. The 220-gr. .30/06 has a muzzle velocity of 2,410, muzzle energy of 2,810.

Now, ballistics figures aren't the sole criterion of killing power, by a long way. Other factors — bullet weight, shape, caliber, construction — have a bearing. If the .45/70 is a better elk cartridge than the .30/06, then the 1910 Apperson has it all over a new Cadillac. If the 405-gr. .45/70 slug does as much damage to an elk (or any other animal) as the 180-gr. .30/06 bullet, then my name is Fu Wong Chung. I might add, since I've seen game killed with a .45/70 as well as with a .30/06, that I'm not exactly a mere theorist.

Four .30/06 rifles: At top is a restocked Springfield, originally Army surplus. Below it is O'Connor's pet—a .30/06 based on an F.N. (Belgian) Mauser action with Sukalle barrel. Second from bottom is Remington's Model 721, a light rifle. At bottom is the Model 70 Winchester. All are effective on any American big game.

Many other citizens have shot more game with the .30/06 than I have, but I believe I've done enough hunting with rifles chambered for that cartridge to have more than a fair idea about its capabilities. I started shooting a .30/06 back in 1914 when I was a bright-eyed lad of 12, and I've been using .30/06 rifles ever since. I have shot the little Southwestern wild pigs, called javelinas, with the .30/06 — and

18

they weigh about 40 to 50 lb. on the hoof. I have also shot Alaska moose with it, and they weigh 1,500 lb. or more. With the .30/06 I have killed six grizzlies, a couple of elk, assorted mule and white-tail deer, black bears, antelope, caribou, and mountain sheep.

A big bull mountain caribou doesn't miss being as large as a bull elk by very much, and I once polished off two such bulls with three shots — all hits — at right around 400 yd. with the humble .30/06 and the 180-gr. Remington pointed soft-point Core-Lokt bullet. My first shot, from the prone position, hit one bull right through the lungs. He ran about 10 yd. and fell. I swung over to the second bull, fired, and heard the bullet strike. He ran about 30 yd. and stopped. I shot again and he went down with both shoulders broken. The second shot was, I believe, unnecessary. Those two bulls lay dead not 50 yd. apart. Why? As in *any* big-game shooting, placement of shots is vastly more important than the bullet used. Those caribou went down because they were hit right, whereas if they'd been shot in the paunch with a .375 Magnum they would probably have given me a long chase.

One of the hot-stove-league arguments now going on is whether the .30/06 or the .270 is the better big-game cartridge. I have hunted for years with both calibers. Right now I have three .30/06's and three .270's. And that, I believe, shows how I feel.

As I see it, the 200-foot-seconds-greater velocity of the 130-gr. .270 factory load gives it a *slight* edge over the 150-gr. .30/06 on lighter animals like deer, antelope, and sheep. This .270 load also has a some-what longer point-blank range, 275 yd. or thereabouts when the rifle is sighted in to put the bullet 4 in. high at 200. The point-blank range would be 250 yd. in the .30/06. A somewhat higher impact velocity at the longer ranges gives the .270, I believe, a higher percentage of instant kills than the .30/06. Flatter trajectory plus slightly less pun-ishing recoil means that many hunters can do more accurate shooting with the .270.

On the other hand, the .30/06's heavier bullets make it a little superior on the larger animals. So while it's my belief that the .270 has the edge on lighter game, I'd give the .30/06 the nod on heavier animals. I doubt that anything that can be put through a .270 would be quite as effective on the heavier stuff as a good 180-gr. bullet in the .30/06. And when a man is hunting really heavy and potentially dangerous game I don't think any .270 load is as effective as a good 220-gr. bullet in the .30/06, as these babies play for keeps and the bullet must drive into the vitals at all costs! Friends of mine who have hunted in Africa with the .270 and the .30/06 say the latter's 220-gr. bullet is far better on big game than the .270 with any load.

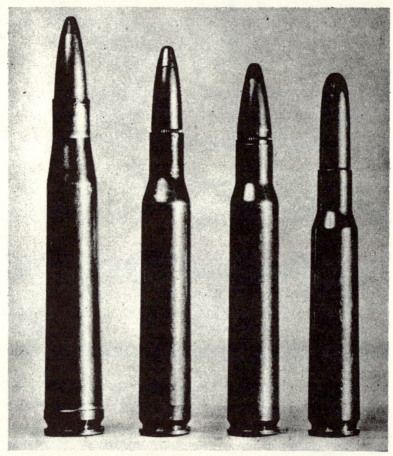

"All-round" big-game cartridges (l. to r.): The powerful (and hard-kicking) .300 H&H Magnum; the .270, which rivals the .30/06 in popularity; the .30/06, still a killing load; and the 7 mm., which has less recoil than the .30/06, almost as much power.

I used to believe — with many another — that the .270 is inherently a more accurate cartridge than the .30/06. And indeed at one time there were more .270 rifles of gilt-edge accuracy than .30/06's of the same class. Now I'm inclined to believe that such accuracy (in either caliber) was due to certain excellent bullets and to individual outstanding rifles. Before the war the only .270's floating around were high-class Model 54 and Model 70 Winchesters, plus some top custom rifles. Contrariwise, there were all sorts and conditions of .30/06's in existence. But today you run across .270's that are good, bad, or indifferent. A good .30/06 is good, and a bum .30/06 is lousy. But the same thing applies to the .270!

Put it this way: any good rifleman can take any North American big-game animal with either the .270 or the .30/06 if he has suitable bullets. If I were hunting antelope in Wyoming I'd prefer the .270, and if I were hunting big Alaska brown bears I'd prefer the .30/06. But if I had to shoot a brownie with a .270, I'd load up with the 160-gr. Barnes bullet and 52 gr. of No. 4350, or simply take the Remington 150-gr. soft-point Core-Lokt factory load and go to it. With that last load, incidentally, I wouldn't feel helpless taking a long shot at a Wyoming antelope.

Part of the criticism of the .30/06 is rooted in the use of unsuitable bullets. For many years I lived in the Southwest, where the most popular game animal is a little white-tail deer whose weight averages about 100 lb. field-dressed. Also on the menu were antelope, which weigh about the same, javelinas that dress out at from 25 to 40 lb., and mule deer that dress out at an average of 200 lb. Most of the hep riflemen who, 20 years ago, used the .30/06 wanted the 150-gr. bullets. Were they easy to get? Brother! The store shelves were loaded with 180 and 220-gr. factory cartridges, but the fast-stepping, quick-opening 150-gr. was hard to come by — practically under-the-counter stuff. When the word got around that a certain store had stocked some ammunition loaded with 150-gr. bullets, the .30/06 fans would rush there and buy a few boxes while the buying was good.

The 150-gr. factory loads at a muzzle velocity of almost 3,000 foot seconds are incomparably the best medicine in the .30/06 for longish ranges on light game like deer, antelope, and sheep. The man behind a scope-sighted .30/06 can carefully sight in to put his group 3 in. high at 100 yd. He'll then be 4 in. high at 200, on the nose at about 250, and 5 in. low at 300. Up to 250 yd. or so, one of those 150-gr. bullets in the chest of a deer-class animal almost always means an instant kill. I have used the old Winchester pointed-expanding bullet in that weight, the U. S. copper tube, the Remington Bronze Point, and the Western open-point. All were good. Of the bunch, the U. S. bullet was the slowest to open, the Western open-point the fastest. Once I shot a coyote with that Western job at no more than 50 yd., and the bullet didn't even get through to the far side. The inside of the coyote was a mush. I saw a friend smack a running white-tail buck in the neck, and that fast-opening bullet almost took the whole neck off.

For animals of this class the 150-gr. bullets are the quickest killers in the .30/06, and offer the best chance to anchor game with poorly placed shots. Out at and beyond 200 yd. they'll usually knock a deer down and keep him down, while the heavier, slower 180-gr. bullet often puts a deer down only to let him get up and run anywhere from 25 to 200 yd.

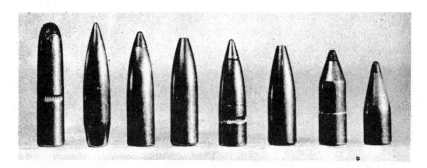

Some .30/06 bullets, left to right: 220-gr. soft-point Remington Core Lokt, for very heavy game like moose or Alaska brown bear; 180-gr. boattail, for match shooting; 180-gr. spitzer speer, a soft-point for all-round use; 172-gr. Western Tool & Copper Works open-point; 150-gr. Remington Bronze Point; 150-gr. Western Tool & Copper Works open-point; 150-gr. 2-D, Modern Gun Shop; and 110-gr. Speer.

If 150-gr. ammunition for the .30/06 had been well distributed in the Southwest, I doubt that the .270 would have had its tremendous popularity there. But when lads using the 180-gr. .30/06 stuff saw someone with a .270 reach out and bounce a big buck at 300 yd., they'd naturally be impressed. The .270 owes its rise to fame and fortune in the mountain states to the fact that in spite of hell and high water you simply could not, for many years, get any other ammunition than that loaded with excellent 130-gr. bullets. If its original load had been the 150-gr. bullet at 2,800 foot seconds, it would have become about as popular as the 7 mm.

The 180-gr. load is the best *all-round* cartridge in the .30/06. It does pretty well on white-tails and such, but don't let anyone tell you that it gives as high a percentage of instantaneous kills as the 150-gr. .30/06 bullet or the 130-gr. .270. Most 180-gr. bullets are constructed to hold together. That kind of construction, plus the moderate impact velocity of the 180-gr. bullets, simply does not permit the blasting effect produced by the fragmentation of lighter, faster bullets. The 180-gr. bullet does better on larger animals, like elk and big bull caribou, simply because they have more bulk to slow up the bullet and permit it to expand into a flesh-shattering slug.

I mentioned the quick kills on those two bull caribou. On the same trip I shot a big Dall ram in the upper part of the lungs, and he stayed on his feet, giving no sign of having been hit, for five or six seconds before he toppled over. I shot a desert sheep through the lungs with a 180-gr. .30/06 bullet and he too seemed unhit. Because the shot was an easy one and I didn't see how I could have missed, I hunted for him in the rocks and found him about 25 yd. from where I'd last seen him. The 150-gr. bullet would have killed him in his tracks.

The .30/06's 150-gr. bullet is deadly on animals of the elk class if the hunter has a good broadside shot. But if the animal is in a position where the shoulder has to be broken, or a good deal of tissue penetrated before the vital area is struck, the 180-gr. is more effective.

Once I deliberately tried to break a big bull caribou's shoulder at about 170 yd. with the 150-gr. bullet. The bullet went to pieces in the shoulder with a noise that sounded like a firecracker going off, but it didn't even knock the bull off his feet. Most 180-gr. .30/06 bullets would have gone clear through without any such shattering effect. I sent the next bullet through the upper lungs and that was the end of the caribou.

I have a .30/06 that's my pride and joy. I cherish it because it will send 'most any weight bullet of the same point of impact at 200 yd. The rifle weighs 9¼ lb., with sling, Lyman Alaskan scope on a Griffin & Howe mount, and full magazine. It is built on a Fabrique Nationale (Belgian) Mauser action with a Sukalle barrel and a twist of

1 in 12 in., and it has a superb stock by Alvin Biesen. When I go out for both light and heavy game, I take along 150-gr. and 180-gr. ammunition. The 150-gr. stuff is sighted in to hit on the nose at 250 yd., the 180 at 225. At 200 yd. both bullets shoot into the same group, the 150-gr. bullet landing slightly higher than the 180.

When I am hunting sheep with the 150-gr. stuff, and glass a grizzly, I simply shift to the 180-gr. bullets and begin to stalk. I've shot six grizzlies with the 180-gr., and since I haven't got eaten up by one yet, the old .30/06 must be at least adequate.

After my experience, particularly with the Remington 180-gr. pointed soft-point Core-Lokt .30/06 bullet, I've concluded there's no need in America for a bullet giving greater penetration. In the Yukon I once put four of those bullets, rapid fire, right behind the shoulder of a big, rangy grizzly that measured 7 ft. 7 in. from tip of nose to tip of tail as it lay dead. The bear was on a sandbar, and every bullet fired went clear through him and cracked against rocks on the far side.

For years the favorite brown-bear medicine of Hosea Sarber, noted Alaska game warden and guide, was the 172-gr. bullet of the Western Tool & Copper Works; it was loaded for a muzzle velocity of about 2,750 foot seconds. Since Sarber felt that the load was adequate, and since he's killed more grizzlies than I have ever seen, I'm going to take his word for it.

For North American hunting, the 220-gr. bullet hasn't much place in the scheme of things, I believe, unless it is for Alaska brown bears. Since they're often shot at close range and in the alders, when high velocity is of no particular moment, and where the bullet would have to drive through heavy chest muscles, I can see that the 220-gr. Silvertips and Core-Lokts would be the business.

If a man wants a bullet that will go clear through a moose on a broadside shot, the 220-gr. is also good; but this is hearsay on my part, for the only 220-gr. .30/06 bullet I ever shot at a moose very definitely didn't go clear through, although it did break a shoulder on the way in. There's something to be said for the 220-gr. in timber shooting — the heavy, round-nose bullets are deflected less by brush than a lighter bullet with sharper profile.

For the heaviest African antelope, like the eland, or for knocking over big Bengal tigers or stopping charging African lions, the 220-gr. bullets make the .30/06 a real rifle. Stewart Edward White used the

24

.30/06 on dozens of lions, his bullets being the old Remington 220-gr. delayed mushroom and the Western 220-gr. boattail with only a pinpoint of lead exposed. He felt that for this work, the .30/06 so loaded was superior to the .405 Winchester. And yet I hear tell it's not suitable for elk!

This big caribou bull was running when O'Connor hit it behind the shoulder with a 180-gr. Core-Lokt bullet, pointed soft-point, from his .30/06. It dropped within 10 yd.

Curiously enough, the most accurate load I ever used in a .30/06 (and one of the most accurate I've ever run across in any rifle) was the now-discontinued Western 220-gr. pinpoint boattail with 52 gr. of du Pont No. 4350 powder. With that load a man could shoot an elephant's eye out at 100 yd. With it I shot many groups of less than a minute of angle. In fact, I was so fascinated by its astonishing accuracy in an old Springfield of mine that I used up my small supply of bullets in group shooting.

The 220-gr. bullets, because of their round noses and moderate velocity, should be the choice for elk and moose in brush and timber, since they are less likely to deflect. But under no circumstances should they be used on light game like deer, because — except for the old-fashioned soft-points, which had a lot of lead exposed — they do not open up fast enough to inflict a quick-killing wound. Few hunters would go after really heavy game, such as elephant, rhinoceros, and

25

Cape buffalo, with a .30/06; but if it had to be done I suppose the best bet would be a full-metal-case bullet, and one has never been loaded for sporting purposes in this country.

In the past, 170-gr. bullets have been loaded for the .30/06 but I can't see any great advantage in them. Likewise I don't think the 200-gr. bullet is sufficiently superior to the 180-gr. to pay to load it, although I used the 200-gr. Barnes bullet with 56 gr. of No. 4350, and found it powerful and accurate.

Long ago, for lighter game, I settled on 53 of No. 4320 with the 150-gr. bullet. That combination has given me good accuracy, long case life, and satisfactory killing power. And it shoots to the same point of impact as the Remington factory load with the 150-gr. Bronze Point bullet. Muzzle velocity is probably about 2,925 to 2,950 foot seconds, and pressure below 50,000 pounds to the square inch.

With the 180-gr. bullet, 49.5 gr. of the same powder is a good bet. Likewise 56 gr. of No. 4350.

For some reason most .30/06 rifles will put the 220 and 180-gr. factory loads pretty much to the same point of impact at 100 yd., but they will toss the 150-gr. from 5 to 7 in. higher. For that reason a .30/06 that — because of bedding or barrel contour — will lay everything pretty much to the same point of impact is one to be cherished and used sparingly.

Lads getting custom rifles might well specify a 1-in-12 twist, which stabilizes even the 220-gr. bullets over game ranges and which will give very good accuracy with 125-gr. bullets if a .30/06 owner *has* to use his rifle on varmints.

All in all, I question whether most hunters need much more rifle than the .30/06 on any North American big game. I do not think cartridge progress stopped with the .30/06 by any means, but it still is a most excellent cartridge. No doubt the .375 H.&H. Magnum will give more quick kills on the larger game. So will the powerful, blown-out .300 Magnums like the Weatherby, Ackley, Mashburn, and Pfeifer Magnums.

But in the .30/06 you find about all the recoil that most men can handle, and no one who is afraid of his rifle's recoil can shoot it well. It is far better to put in a well-placed shot with a .30/06 than a poorly placed shot with a shoulder-jolting .375. For the record, the recoil of a .30/06 Winchester Model 70 with the 180-gr. bullet is 17 foot pounds, whereas that of the .375 with the 300-gr. bullet is almost twice as much — 33.6 foot pounds. Some riflemen claim they can shoot a .375 for fun. I can't. I believe, too, that a hunter should *enjoy* shooting his big-game rifle; if it punishes him he'll never get enough practice to become a deadly shot.

I am further convinced that reported lack of killing power in the .30/06 stems from poor shooting or unsuitable bullets — things that the finest cartridges in the world are not proof against.

Obviously, a man who shoots but one box of ammunition a year can't be a very good shot, and he wouldn't be good with any caliber. Nor can you use moose bullets on deer, or woodchuck bullets on moose, and expect quick kills. Use the *right* bullet for the game you hunt, practice enough so that you can place your shot accurately, and the .30/06 won't let you down.

The .30/06 is a popular and widely used caliber, so it follows that a lot of game must surely escape wounded after being hit with .30/06 bullets. But it also follows that if the same number of hunters used the .375 Magnum or even the .470 Nitro Express — and shot as poorly — they would also lose a lot of game.

In times past the .30/06 was over-sold. I don't think it is the answer to every need. The man who wants one rifle for both varmints and deer-size game is better off with a .250/3000 or a .257. For medium-size game at long ranges and for varmints like coyotes I think the .270 has a small edge. The recoil sensitive shooter who wants to hunt all North American game is better off with the authoritative but mild 7 mm. For the very longest ranges, the .300 Magnum and the fine .270 and 7 mm. Magnum wildcats have a distinct edge.

But with its moderate recoil, its readily available ammunition in a variety of bullet weights, its power, and its accuracy, the .30/06 is one of the world's great big-game cartridges.

CHAPTER III

The Worldwide .375 Magnum

**Big game throughout the world falls
before this cartridge which is
gaining in popularity**

J UST as the .30/06 is a great all-round cartridge for North America — one that can be used in a pinch on woodchucks and (also in a pinch) on Alaska brown bear — the .375 Holland & Holland Magnum is the all-round *world* cartridge. If a rifleman had to, he could hunt successfully every one of the world's big-game animals with it, everything from the 40-lb. Southwestern javelina and the little European roebuck, to the Asiatic tiger, Alaska brown bear, and elephant.

Our hunter might not have very much roebuck left after hitting it with a .375. And he might wish for more bullet weight if he got into a rhubarb with an elephant. Nevertheless, the .375 does pretty well for anything. With the 270-gr. bullet at a muzzle velocity of over 2,700 foot seconds, it has a flat enough trajectory for a 300-yd. shot at an Asiatic ibex or a North American bighorn sheep, plus enough crushing knockdown power to set a charging African Cape buffalo back on his rump.

All this is the *majority* opinion. There is a minority that considers the .375 Magnum neither fish nor fowl, and declares that it's too heavy for a mountain rifle, kicks too much for accurate shooting at long range, and doesn't have enough knockdown power in the clutch when the hunter is faced with really dangerous game.

There seems to be very little neutral ground as far as the .375 is concerned. It is almost as controversial a cartridge as the .220 Swift and the .270 W.C.F. It is the darling of the small but highly articulate group of big-bore, heavy-bullet boys, who claim that no animal larger than a mule deer should be shot with a rifle of .30 caliber or less, or with a bullet weighing less than 250-gr.

Roy Weatherby poses with a rough, tough African buffalo he downed with his custom .375 magnum.

The more extreme members of this school even advocate the .375 as a deer rifle, claiming that the big Magnum slug will smack a deer for a loop much more efficiently than will lighter, faster bullets such as the 130-gr. and the 150-gr. .30/06, and yet actually destroy less meat. I have never been able to follow that reasoning, since it's been my experience that killing power and the ability to make a large wound are closely related.

Conservative American hunters are inclined to believe that the real field for the .375 is the Old World, where game runs larger and shorter-tempered than in North America, and that if Old Nonesuch is to be used in this country, its natural prey is the very biggest stuff — Alaska brown bear, polar bear, and the largest Alaska moose in heavy timber.

No matter who is right, the massive fact remains that the .375 is growing in popularity. Ten or 15 years ago, only the largest sporting-goods stores in the largest cities stocked .375 rifles and ammunition. Ask the average small-town dealer in those days for .375 ammunition and he'd give you the kind of look a hamburger-stand attendant would toss at a customer who demanded an omelet with truffles and a bottle of Château Rimaud, 1914.

Ain't so today! In doing my leg work for this article, I asked a dealer in an Idaho town of 12,000 if he ever sold any .375 rifles. It turned out that he had peddled no less than four in a year, and that he has a half a dozen on hand he hopes to press into the sweaty little hands of eager elk hunters even now. He always stocks .375 ammunition. And so it is elsewhere. The .375 is coming along.

The cartridge is no Johnny-come-lately, having been around since 1912, when it was introduced by the famous British gunmaking firm of Holland & Holland. It is based on a long belted case, one which has the advantages of the rimless case in that it works easily through the staggered Mauser-type magazine, plus the advantages of the rimmed case in that headspace is shorter and easier to control. (In a rimless case headspace runs from the face of the bolt to the shoulder of the case; in a belted case it runs from the face of the bolt to the forward edge of the belt.) Holland & Holland also based their Super .30 (which we know as the .300 H & H Magnum) and their .257 Magnum on the belted case.

The case is used by other British manufacturers, as it was by a few German manufacturers before the war. In this country a whole flock of wildcats, such as the Weatherby series, are based on it. Wildcatters dearly love the case because of its larger powder capacity and the great strength toward the head afforded by the belt.

In this country we think of the .375 as the *only* .375. In reality it is but one of many. Actually the caliber name is based on groove diameter, as is the .257, and not on bore diameter, as in the case of the .270, .30/06, .300 Savage, .35 Remington, and other cartridges. Bore diameter of .375 Magnum barrels as cut by Winchester is actually .366, groove diameter, .376. Winchester uses a six-groove barrel with a groove width of .115 in. and a twist of 1-12. If we followed the usual practice of naming a caliber from the bore diameter of the barrel, the

.375 would actually be a .36, but .375 sounds more formidable. Nearest native American cartridge to it is the old .38/55, with its groove diameter of .378.

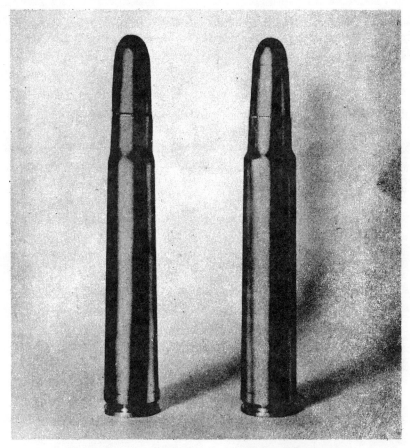

Normal .375 cartridge (left) and the .375 Weatherby. Greater powder content of the latter gives bullet increased velocity.

First ".375" was the 9.5 mm. Mannlicher-Schoenauer, which came out in 1910. The British restocked M-S rifles for the .375 cartridge, and also built rifles for it on Mauser actions labeling them ".375 Rimless Nitro Express." Following the usual European custom of having a rimmed counterpart of a rimless cartridge — so that the same ballistics can be obtained in single-shot and double-barreled rifles as in magazine rifles — the British brought out a cartridge known as the .375 Flanged (meaning rimmed) Nitro Express.

The 9.5, the renamed .375 rimless, and the rimmed job all used 270-gr. bullets at muzzle velocities of from 2,000 to 2,150 foot seconds, and with muzzle energies of from 2,340 to 2,750 foot pounds. All were nice for medium game in timber, but not for really dangerous game. Now and then a secondhand Holland & Holland double rifle marked .375 Flanged Nitro Express turns up at a moderate price, and some sucker falls on it with glad cries, thinking he's caught himself a rifle for the .375 Magnum. But it's the old job for the rimmed counterpart of the original 9.5 mm.

Actually the rimmed running mate of the .375 H. & H. Magnum is known as the .375 Flanged Magnum. It has a rimmed case about like that of the standard .375 Magnum, as we know it. British ammunition people (who, unlike American loading companies, make no secret of how much powder they use and what pressures they get) load the .375 Flanged Magnum with a bit less powder, thus getting less velocity and less pressure.

The 300-gr. bullet in the rimmed version for doubles attains a muzzle velocity of 2,424 foot seconds with 56 gr. of Cordite powder; the belted rimless form for magazine rifles, with 58 gr. of Cordite, produces 2,500 foot seconds, according to British figures.

Holland & Holland now makes double rifles particularly for the American market, chambering them for the belted-rimless .375 as we know it, and "regulated" for the American loads.

The first .375 Magnums were built by H. & H. on Magnum Mauser actions imported from Germany. Such actions are of the Model 98 type, but are about ½ in. longer than the standard 98 action. As far as I know, the receiver ring is always of the same size. All actions I have seen have a square bridge and hinged floorplate, with release button in the forward portion of the trigger guard.

From the first, the British loaded three weights of bullets — 235 gr., at a muzzle velocity of 2,800 foot seconds; 270 gr. (the original) at 2,650; and 300 gr. at 2,500. In rifles with good stiff barrels they all shoot to pretty much the same point of impact, usually the 235-gr. bullet landing highest, the 300-gr. lowest.

The first .375 I played with, a Model 70 Winchester, would put all three weights in a 3-in. circle at 100 yd. When I sighted in to put the

270-gr. bullet on the nose at 200 yd., the 235-gr. hit around 2½ in high at that range and on the nose at about 250 yd.; the 300-gr. hit about 3 in. low at 250.

Any .375 Magnum load produces recoil that's a bit heavy for the finest precision shooting, but if a man can handle such recoil, the Magnum is a fine mountain rifle with both the 235 and the 270-gr. bullet.

H. & H.'s new .375 was a quick sellout. On African game it soon became more popular than such famous all-round rifles as the .404 Rimless Nitro Express and the .416 Rigby, which move 400-gr. bullets at 2,125 and 2,300 foot seconds, respectively. To a great extent it also displaced medium-bore doubles like the .450/.400 — a .40 caliber bullet in a .45 case. Hunting Britishers have used the .375 all over the world, on everything from wild sheep in India to elephants in Africa. Almost all English authorities recommend it as *the* all-round rifle.

The first American .375's, also made on Magnum Mauser actions, were custom jobs by such firms as the late Hoffman Arms Co. of Ardmore, Okla., the late Niedner Rifle Corp., of Dowagiac, Mich., and the much-alive Griffin & Howe, of New York City. In addition Stoeger Arms Corp., also of New York, imported some British Webley & Scott .375's built on the German Magnum action. The Western Cartridge Co. brought out .375 ammunition in the early 1920's.

However, the .375 Magnum remained a luxury to most American hunters until 1937, when Winchester, in unveiling its famous Model 70, made it available not only in the common or garden-variety calibers like .30/06 and .270, but in the .375 and .300 Magnums. That meant you could get yourself a .375 for around $65.

The big brass of Winchester were surprised at how many .375's were sold, and I believe they are surprised at the number being sold today. The way the big guns move, you'd think rhinos were chasing kindergarten kids home in Westport, Conn., and brown bears were knocking over garbage cans in the backyards of Walla Walla, Wash.

Since the great Mauser-Werke in Germany, which made the big Magnum Mauser actions have been destroyed, the British today build their .375's around Model 1917 Enfield actions and on regular Model 98 or F. N. (Belgian) Mauser actions that have been milled out for the longer cartridge and to which special magazine assemblies with long boxes have been fitted. American custom gunsmiths build .375's around the same actions.

The American who wants a .375, unless he has something exceedingly special in mind, is probably wise to lay his wampum on the line and catch himself a Model 70. He then has a very fine, smooth action designed especially for the Magnum cartridges, a good, correctly bored, rifled, and chambered barrel, a good low bolt and a good safety.

If he wants to be a bit fancy he can get a Model 70 in the good-looking super grade, and if he wants to go hog wild he can have the rifle remodeled by a custom gunsmith. My own .375 has been restocked in fine French walnut, adjusted, and equipped with scope sight and Lyman 48 receiver sight by Griffin & Howe.

Three .375's. Top is a custom-made Weatherby magnum. Weatherby and other gunmakers fit .375 barrels to Mauser (F.N. and Model 98) and 1917 Enfield actions. Center is the standard Winchester Model 70 in .375 with an open sight. This gun brings the big cartridge within the range of the average shooter. Below is a Model 70 restocked by Griffin & Howe. A Stith 2¾X Bear Cub scope is added.

There are plenty of good gunsmiths who can build a .375 from scratch on an F. N. Mauser or a Model 1917 Enfield action, giving the owner any barrel length, contour, or type of stock he desires.

Because of its very husky recoil, a .375 should, in my opinion, weigh not less than 9 lb., and 10 lb. might be better. The standard Winchester Model 70 weighs about 9 lb. with iron sights. My own restocked job comes to 10½ lb. complete with scope, sling, and three cartridges in the magazine.

Not long ago I heard from a gunsmith who was building himself a .375 to weigh just 7½ lb., complete with scope. With it he was going to hunt elk and — of all things — mule deer. There's a musket which, as far as I am concerned, he can keep. Even a 10-lb. .375 has a lot of wallop on the butt-end, and a featherweight in the caliber would knock you from under your hat.

Not only is the .375 often used on heavy game, and in Africa on dangerous game, but it's also often used in heavy brush which sometimes gets very, very wet, therefore it seems to me the best sighting equipment for it is a good, rugged scope of from 2¼X to 2¾X on a quick-detachable side mount, plus a receiver sight with a quick-detachable slide, such as the Lyman 48. My own restocked Model 70 has the 48 and a Stith 2¾X scope, with double adjustments, on the Griffin & Howe side mount. The scope is mounted as low as it is possible to get it. But Phil Johnstone and Seymour Griffin of Griffin & Howe tell me that many of the scopes they mount on .375's, particularly for African use, are set high enough so the receiver sight can be left on and used *beneath* the scope.

Stock for the .375 should have but little more drop at heel than at comb, so that recoil comes straight back. In mine, drop at heel is exactly the same as that at comb. The rifle was, of course, stocked for iron sights, which means that the withdrawn bolt clears the point of the comb by about ¼ in. The stock is perfect for iron sights and not bad for steady holding with the scope.

If anything, the stock on a .375 should be a bit longer (perhaps ¼ in.) than one on a rifle with the recoil of the .30/06 — also to minimize recoil. The stock would always be equipped with a rubber recoil pad. A .375 with a short, crooked stock, particularly if the comb is too high and too thick, will beat you to death. A good stock cuts down the apparent recoil, but never let it be said that the .375 — even with the best stock, plus adequate weight — isn't a kicker!

Let's look at some figures. A .30/06 cartridge pushing the standard 180-gr. bullet along at 2,700 foot seconds, and fired in a rifle weighing about 8 lb., has 17.5 foot pounds of free recoil. A .270 rifle of similar weight, shooting the 130-gr. bullet, has 14.3 foot pounds of free recoil. The .348 with the 200-gr. bullet has 22.6 foot pounds, and the .300 Magnum with the 180-gr. bullet at 2,900 has a bit more. The .375 with the 300-gr. bullet has 33.6 foot pounds, or almost twice the free recoil of the .30/06 with the most commonly used load. Some years ago du Pont ballisticians, after working up figures on free recoil with various shotgun loads in guns of different weights, commented that "recoil heavier than 28 foot pounds cannot be endured for any considerable time."

So don't let anyone tell you that the .375 doesn't kick. Getting rid of those heavy large-diameter bullets at relatively high speed is bound to produce kick, particularly in a light rifle. When a .375 is fired the rifle comes back fast, and the head of the shooter snaps back as though Sugar Ray Robinson had just hung one on his chin. Not long ago Raymond Speer and I were chronographing some factory loads from a bench rest. Because I am a generous fellow I didn't want to hog the gun, so after five shots I turned it over to Raymond to shoot. Every time that cannon boomed his head flashed back so fast it was hard to see. It was like the snapper on the end of a whip.

What is the effect of this husky recoil? When you're shooting from prone or from a bench rest, with the body solidly behind the rifle, it isn't pleasant. To get good groups then, I have to space my shots out and make a special effort to concentrate on my hold while I squeeze the trigger off gently. When you shoot from the sitting position, recoil is much less disturbing, and from offhand it isn't bad at all. In shooting at game, particularly large, tough, disagreeable game that might come hunking over and grab a piece out of your leg, the recoil of a .375 probably wouldn't bother anyone.

The .375 is a *big-game rifle*. It isn't a varmint rifle, and although most .375's give accuracy comparable to that of the .30/06, it isn't a target rifle. I can take a .375 and from the sitting position stay pretty well inside a 10-in. bull at 200 yd. for the first five shots. After that, as much as I hate to admit it, I begin getting some 4's as the recoil effect builds up. But it isn't often that anyone is going to shoot more than two or three shots at big game, particularly with the .375, which bears the reputation of smacking them down. Some citizens dote on shooting the .375, and claim that doing so fills their souls with bliss. At some risk of being called a sissy, I'll admit that my recoil tolerance is about 25 foot pounds, and when a rifle belts me around with more push than that, shooting it becomes something of a chore.

The Western Cartridge Co. loads the 270-gr. bullet in the .375 to a muzzle velocity of 2,700 foot seconds and the astounding muzzle energy of 4,440 foot pounds. It loads the 300-gr. bullet to 2,580 and 4,435. The .404 and .416 rimless Nitro Express cartridges, which even the British admit are O.K. for elephants, turn up only slightly more energy. The 235-gr. bullet, which the British push along at 2,800 foot seconds, is no longer loaded commercially in the United States. I doubt that there's any need for a flatter-shooting load for the .375 than the 270-gr. In trajectory it shoots like the .30/06's 180-gr., since their muzzle velocities are the same, and the sectional densities of the two bullets are practically identical — .270 for a 180-gr. .30/06 as against .274 for the 270-gr. .375 bullet. The 300-gr. .375 bullet has somewhat less sectional density than the 220-gr. .30 caliber job, approximating that of a 200-gr. .30 caliber bullet. Trajectory of the 300-gr. is sufficiently flat to sight in for 200 yd. and get a rise of a bit less than 3 in. above line of scope sight at 100 yd.

The 270-gr. bullet is made only in semipointed soft-point style. With its flat trajectory, great mass, and tremendous knockdown power, it is undoubtedly the best .375 bullet for any of the more massive North American animals, such as the Alaska brown bear, Alaska moose, polar bear, and walrus. It is the best bullet for African plains game, and if a man should feel himself coming down with a yen to hunt sheep or elk with the .375, this 270-gr. bullet should be his pigeon. Western makes the 300-gr. bullet not only in the expanding Silvertip style but in a full-metal-case bullet, or "solid," especially designed for African hunting. Some years ago there were squawks about the Silvertip's opening up too fast, but apparently Western has stiffened up its core and jacket and cured the trouble.

The .375 Magnum isn't a handloader's pet because lads who buy .375's are usually not accuracy nuts, chuck hunters or bench-rest shooters. When they touch one off, it is usually at something that sheds hair and leaks blood. However, .375 dies are obtainable for most loading tools; Barnes and Modern Gun Shop make bullets; and the big cartridge is nice to handload. One can duplicate factory ballistics or load down to a very pleasant deer medicine, using the 255-gr. .38/55 bullet at about 2,000 foot seconds.

A variation of the .375 cartridge of particular interest to the handloader is the .375 Weatherby Magnum, which is the standard .375

case fire-formed in a Weatherby chamber to sharper shoulder and greater powder capacity. Weatherby, using from 88 to 90 gr. of No. 4350 powder with the 300-gr. bullet, steps muzzle velocity up to between 2,750 and 2,800 foot seconds, and muzzle energy to over 5,000 foot pounds — ballistically similar to the run-of-the-mine British Nitro Express elephant cartridges.

Strictly for Big game (with a capital B) the .375 Magnum is probably the most versatile of all the world's cartridges. If a man doesn't mind lugging around a fairly heavy rifle, the .375 is accurate and flat-shooting enough for mountain game, and powerful enough for dangerous game at close quarters. If one rifle is to be taken on an African safari, outfitters recommend that it be a .375; and if two or more rifles are taken, one should be a .375. Many American guides in the Alaskan brown-bear country use .375's to protect their dudes in emergencies. One wrote me he could probably kill any brownie that ever walked with a .30/06, but having a .375 in his mitts filled him with confidence and made his dudes feel safe.

The .375 should be a beauty for longish shots on elk, on moose above timberline, or on grizzly, but only if the man behind it can handle the recoil and shoot his big Magnum accurately. Good way to find out is to try some practice shots at 200 yd. — five from offhand, five from sitting, and five from prone. Then try the same strings with a .30/06 or a .270.

If you find that your 15 shots compare favorably with the 15 fired from the less powerful rifle, mostly 5's with only a few close 4's — then you're justified in hunting with the .375. If, on the other hand, you group, say, the .30/06 bullets pretty well in and around the bull, but scatter half your .375 shots all over the target, then you'd better retire Big Bertha until you can shoot her better.

No matter how big, how powerful, how impressive a rifle is, it still cannot be counted on to kill consistently with a poorly placed shot. Break a front leg with a .375 and you have just broken a leg — you aren't any closer to getting your elk than if you had broken it with a .30/30!

CHAPTER IV

The Best Shotgun Gauge

**What it is depends on a lot of factors
analyzed here**

AT this late date it's no secret that shotgun gauges get their names from the number of pure-lead balls of bore diameter that it takes to make a pound. There are ten 10 gauge balls in a pound, twelve 12 gauge, and so on. The one exception is the .410, which isn't a gauge at all, but a caliber, and measured in thousandths of an inch. If the .410 were named like the others it would be 67½ gauge. The gauge system began, I believe, in England, but it is used wherever shotguns are manufactured. The British, however, usually say "bore" instead of "gauge" — for instance, a "10 bore." And some continental guns bear such markings as "Cal. 12."

In any event, bore gauges are standard all over the world, and if chamber length is correct, American shot shells can be used in foreign guns and foreign ammunition in American guns.

It's interesting to note that the gauges were established before the days of choke boring. For that reason a 12 gauge ball cannot be used in a 12 gauge gun; for while it would fit the bore, it would be too small for the muzzle, where the choke is. Consequently, shotgun ball cartridges in 12 gauge are loaded with balls that would run about 14 to the pound, and 16 gauge ball cartridges with balls that run around 18 to the pound.

In muzzle-loading days, guns were also built in 4 and 6 gauge, but I have never seen a breechloader larger than 8 gauge. In early breech-loading days the 10 gauge was the standard gun, and the man who used a 12 gauge was considered a small-bore addict and a daring and reckless fellow. The real wildfowl gun was the 8 gauge. When I was a kid an uncle of mine had a cherished 8 gauge Greener with hammers and Damascus barrels and I was dying to shoot it. I finally sneaked it out and shot a couple of mallards on a pothole with it. That ponderous cannon kicked me back 3 ft. and sent up a cloud of gray smoke so dense that seconds passed before I could see the cadavers of my two puddle ducks floating on the water.

It's possible that 14 and 18 gauge breechloading shotguns have been made in the United States, but I've never seen one. They have been made in Europe, though, and every now and then someone will ask me to identify one of them. Muzzle-loaders in those gauges were quite common in earlier times.

Several factors put the skids under the 8 gauge. For one thing, 8 gauge guns were heavy, clumsy clubs that were difficult to carry, swing, and shoot. Secondly, choke boring and better ammunition came along, and a great charge of shot was no longer needed to get good pattern density for long-range kills. Finally, the big guns were outlawed by the federal government for use on migratory birds, just prior to the first World War. Today 8 gauge shells are unobtainable.

The fate of the 8 has pretty much overtaken the 10. Through the 1880's and 1890's the 12 gauge began to displace the 10 in upland shooting because it was lighter, handier, and for the most part just as effective. As interest in the 10 waned, the loading companies paid less attention to its ammunition, and for years the only 10 gauge shells obtainable were loaded with 1¼ oz. of shot, the same amount carried in maximum 12 gauge loads. The curious old Winchester Model 1901 lever-action repeating shotguns were made in 10 gauge, but the more popular and handier Model 1897 and Model 1912 guns were not — and that helped to accelerate the downfall of the 10.

Prior to the last war there was a slight survival of interest in the 10. High-speed loads with 1⅝ oz. of shot in standard 2⅞-in. cases became available and stepped up the power of the 10. However, the loads were unsafe in many of the older guns, particularly those with twist or Damascus barrels. Furthermore, the same amount of shot was available in the 3-in. 12 gauge Magnum shell, which came into being about the same time. Along in the 1930's the Western Cartridge Co. pioneered the 3½-in. 10 gauge Magnum shell (which was, as far as

40

shot charge went, really an 8 gauge making like a 10) and both Ithaca and Parker built doubles for it. This Roman candle used 2 oz. of big shot at high velocity, and the man husky and astute enough to swing and point one of those ponderous 10 gauge Magnums could make kills at astonishing ranges, often knocking a duck out of a flock at 100 yd. or picking off a single at 75 or 80.

But, alas, the demand for those super-10's was small. The fine old Parkers aren't made any more, in 10 or any other gauge. And Ithaca, sad to say, has heeded the siren call of the pump — which is much easier to manufacture — and no longer makes any sort of double. Ammunition in 10 gauge Magnum is still loaded in small quantities.

In reality, the 10 is on the skids now, just as the 8 was 40 or 50 years ago. Less than 1 percent of shot shells sold by the big loading companies are 10 gauge. The handwriting is on the wall!

The gun that has really done all the larger ones to death is the 12, the standard gauge the world over. It's the universal standard for skeet and trap-shooting, the world's favorite water-fowl gun, the world's favorite all-purpose gun, and surely in the United States it's the gun most used in upland hunting. Shells for the 12 gauge Magnum are 3 in. long and loaded like the 10 gauge. The standard upland load, with its 2¾-in. case and 1⅛ oz. of shot, is loaded like a 16. In England the standard 12 upland load has a 2½-in. case and 1 1/16 oz. of shot, and 12 gauge guns are even made to take 2-in. shells loaded with 1 oz. of shot — a 20 gauge load.

More and more the 12 encroaches on the other gauges. Time was when almost all American 12 bore doubles had 30-in. barrels and weighed from 8 to 8½ lb. The pumps and autos were generally heavy and clumsy. Such cannons were not upland guns and they handicapped a man almost as much as if he had a ball and chain on his leg or a midget on his back.

Now the new 12 gauge pumps and automatics are as light as the 16's and 20's used to be. The lightest 12 gauge load available today for upland shooting is the trap load with 1⅛ oz. of No. 7½ or No. 8 shot and 2¾ or 3 drams of powder; and these are just about 16 gauge loads, with approximately the same recoil and report. Thus the new 12's weigh like 16's and 20's, and have recoil-reducing gimmicks that make them like 20's. I wonder what the end result will be.

In England the 12 is even more the universal gauge than in the

United States. The famous London gunmakers turn out 12's as light as 6 lb., with barrels as short as 25 in. No American 12 gauge doubles of that weight have ever been made. That's because the American 12 tends to be an all-round gun, and even our very lightest 12 gauge load has always been a fairly husky one by British standards. Americans have been experimenting with Magnum 12's now for 20 years or more. Fox, Parker, and Smith used to make heavy 12's chambered for 3-in. shells and 1⅜-1⅝ oz. shot, but the Magnums never became very popular until Winchester brought out the Model 12 heavy duck gun for the 3-in. Magnum, which is practically a 10 wearing a 12 gauge label.

The 16 is an excellent all-round gauge and the second most-popular gauge here in the States. On the European continent, where it's far more popular than the 12, it's made not only in doubles but in three-barreled guns and even in those astounding German four-barreled guns.

The standard American chamber — in guns from 20 to 12 gauge — is now 2¾ in., but the standard British chamber is 2½ in. Most European gun chambers are 65 mm. or 2 9/16 in., and are marked, "12-65, 16-65, 20-65." The European equivalent of our 2¾-in. chamber is the 70 mm., and guns with chambers of that length are always so marked. An unmarked chamber is for the shorter shell.

The 16 is an excellent all-round gauge for the man who doesn't want the absolute maximum in range. A full-choke 16 shooting 1⅛ oz. of No. 6 shot should take single ducks to 50 yd., while a full-choke 12 using 1¼ oz. of shot will take them reliably only to about 55 yd., and a Magnum 12 with 1⅝ oz. of shot only to 60 or 65 yd. I said *reliably*.

The maximum 16 gauge load with 1⅛ oz. of shot and 3 drams of powder is about like the standard 12 gauge load. It will kill about as far, kick almost as hard, but make a little less racket.

The 16 is a very pleasant gun to shoot. I like it, but it seems to be my fate never to have one at my disposal. I got a Model 21 Winchester in that gauge, and my wife took it away from me. I acquired another, and was foolish enough to put it up as a stake on the outcome of a round of skeet I shot against one of my sons. I no longer have that 16, or any 16. Guess I'll stick to my 12 gauge Model 21. They'll let Papa keep that one.

A double-barreled 16 gauge can be built with racier, handier lines than a 12, and it can be built lighter. Recoil and muzzle blast are a bit milder, and ammunition is lighter. It is an excellent upland gauge and an excellent all-round gauge. But for skeet or trapshooting the 16 is a definite handicap in competition against 12's, since it uses less shot and produces thinner patterns. A 16 skeet load used in an all-bore event handles only 1 oz. of No. 9 shot as against 1⅛ oz. in a 12.

In the 20 gauge we have another sort of gun — the lightest and trimmest of the real, catch-as-catch-can hunting arms. For the chap who has to walk long distances and lug a gun over hill and dale in upland hunting, the 20 is the business. There is no handsomer, racier-looking gun than a sleek 20 double with 26-in. barrels and beaver-tail fore-end, ejectors, and single trigger. The little 20 pumps are also sweet to handle. Just as the 12 has more range than the 16, the 16 has more range than the 20; but the lighter gun gets on the target faster and thus the handicap is more apparent than real.

Furthermore, a full-choke 20 has about all the range most of us can handle, even on waterfowl. With 1 oz. of No. 6 (about the largest shot that should be used) a good-patterning 20 will take single ducks to a good 45 yd. — and not many gunners can hit them farther away than that with anything. During the early part of the depression things were tough with the O'Connors and I was hard put to keep my wife and young in hog jowl and hoecakes. The family scattergun arsenal was down to two 20 gauge doubles — an L. C. Smith and an Ithaca. It was very seldom that we missed a bird that we would have hit with a 12.

At one time the 20 was loaded with ¾ oz. of shot. Now the "standard" load is ⅞ oz. and the maximum load of the Super-X, Nitro Express type is 1 oz. One big concern has been experimenting with 20 gauge guns chambering 3-in. shells containing 1¼ oz. of shot. Get a load of that! Standard 20 gauge chambers used to be 2½ in., but they were changed to 2¾ in 1926. Many older 20's have 2½ in. chambers, and use of the now-standard American 2¾-in. shells in them raises pressures somewhat and often makes ejection difficult.

The 28 gauge has never been very popular. Parker used to make 28 doubles, and I believe Ithaca also did. The only one currently manu-factured is the Winchester Model 12, used largely in skeet shooting in the small-bore class. The modern 28 gauge shell is loaded with ¾ oz. of shot — the old 20 gauge load. Because the shot column is shorter and pressures are lower, the 28 patterns somewhat better than the .410 and has the edge on it in skeet competition. Chambers of 28 gauge guns were changed from 2½ to 2⅞ in. in 1931.

Let no one think that the 28 is a toy. A citizen with whom I hunt now and then has a Parker DHE-grade 28 with 26-in. barrels, and I have seen him kill cock pheasants that looked as big as bird dogs when they got up. Like 20 gauge ammunition, 28 gauge stuff is light and easy to lug around, a great advantage that the small bores have over the ponderous 12's.

The 28 is a nice little gun, particularly for the young shooter who is recoil-sensitive, but ammunition is poorly distributed and hard to find in many areas. The gauge is too much like the 20 ever to be popular.

The .410 is more popular than the 28, and a vast number of guns have been made in that "gauge," from little pot-metal single-barreled jobs that sold for five bucks or so, through the sleek and handsome little Winchester Model 42, to the flossiest Parker and Ithaca doubles.

Not too many years ago the .410 was made with 2½-in. chambers, and ⅜ oz. of shot was all one could get in its diminutive shell. Even with full choke, its patterns were so thin that kills were difficult beyond 25 yd. Then Winchester brought out the Model 42 pump and the 3-in. shell using ¾ oz. of shot, a move which definitely took the .410 out of the popgun class.

Today's .410 has 2½-in. cases with ½ oz. of shot, and 3-in. cases with ¾-oz. The only use for the ½-oz. load is sub-small-bore skeet shooting. But the ¾-oz. load is practical on game to 30 yd. with No. 7½ and No. 9 shot. Birds frequently are killed with a .410 at well over 30 yd. In August, 1950, Red Earley and I were in the Yukon and Red was hunting blue grouse for the pot with my Model 42. A bird got up at about 40 yd. I yelled for Red not to shoot, but he fired anyway and the big blue hit the ground and never twitched.

Among the many myths about shot-guns is the notion that the smaller the gauge, the smaller the pattern. It ain't so. Exactly the same standards govern the 12, 16, and 20, and a full-choke gun of any of those gauges should put 70 percent of the shot charge into a 30-in. circle at 40 yd. The standard for the .410 is different: a full-choke

.410 should put 70 percent of its pattern inside of a 24-in. circle at 25 yd.

The smaller gauges don't shoot smaller patterns but they do shoot *thinner* patterns, given the same choke and the same amount of shot. That's because the shot column grows longer as gauge decreases, and there is greater shot deformation. That, in turn, decreases the density of the pattern. Actually, there must be a terrific amount of shot deformation in the very long column of the .410 with ¾ oz. of shot, because a .410 pattern simply disintegrates beyond 30 or 35 yd. If you don't believe it, just try patterning a .410 at 40 yd. sometime!

A 12 gauge will handle 1⅛ oz. of shot better than a 16, and 1 oz. of shot better than a 20. The smaller the gauge, the higher the pressures, as a rule; and when pressures are higher, so is the percentage of deformed and useless shot pellets.

Since patterns run thinner in the smaller gauges, they're less effective with larger shot. A full-choke 12 will maintain sufficient pattern density with No. 4's to kill a mallard, say, at 50 yd., but one should probably drop to No. 5's in a 16, and to No. 6's in a 20. With a 28 or a .410, patterns with anything larger than No. 7½'s aren't too hot, and I have had more luck on upland game with No. 9 skeet loads in a .410 than with any other shot size.

As to the relative popularity of the various gauges, one outfit, which does not make a .410, divided its production this way in a recent year : 12 gauge, 52 percent; 16 gauge, 30 percent; and 20 gauge, 17 percent. My own hunch is that now, with the light 12 gauge repeater being sold, figures will swing even more in favor of the larger gauge.

CHAPTER V

Don't Aim a Shotgun

The difference between aiming and
pointing is the difference between
hitting and missing

W HEN we *aim* we see the target in relation to a front sight and a
rear sight. In the case of a shotgun, the rear sight may be the
second bead on the rib or it may be the receiver. When we *point* we
see the target only in relation to the front sight, which may be the
front bead but which is usually the muzzle. Aiming is deliberate;
pointing, on the other hand, is quick and approximate.

The aimer concentrates on his sights. The pointer concentrates on
his target. Let's take two extremes. The handgun man is told that he
cannot shoot high scores unless he pays more attention to the sights
than to the bullseye. And since it's impossible to focus simultaneously
on rear sight, front sight, *and* target, he does his darndest to focus on
his sights; then he sees his bull only as an out-of-focus black blob.

On the other hand, the shotgun shooter should see his target clearly,
be it clay, quail, duck, pheasant, or whatever. Then the muzzle of his
gun — his sight in relation to the target — should be somewhat out
of focus. In fact, some good shotgun handlers believe they do not see
the barrel muzzle at all.

For the last three bird seasons I have done almost all my shooting
with a Winchester Model 21 double with two sets of barrels. One set
is bored modified and improved modified for use on pheasants and
water fowl, and for traps. The other set is bored Skeet No. 1 and Skeet
No. 2 for skeet and quail. The skeet set has a red-bead front sight and

a silver-bead rear sight, and the other set has only a metal front bead.

Actually, it makes no difference whether the front bead is gold, silver, red, blue, or green. Unless I get over-anxious I point, but not with the bead. In fact I pay no attention to it, but point the end of the barrels.

Those who point their guns are fast shots. Those who aim are slow. Fast shots tend to be good; slow shots, poor. When the fast shot slows up he starts missing, as anyone who has shot skeet or traps or watched others shoot can testify. A man will break his targets in a certain "time." When he gets nervous, hesitates, and aims, the spectators know he is going to miss the bird before he shoots.

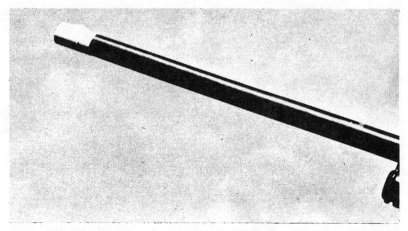

Wrapping the muzzle of a .410 with adhesive tape makes it more conspicuous.

There is one moment, one small part of a second, when the man behind the gun should touch her off. The bird flushes. The hunter's trained muscles bring up the gun. He sees the muzzle in relation to the target. It looks right. He shoots and hits. A good fast upland shot will fire within a couple of seconds after a bird gets out.

Our unskilled shot flushes a bird under similar circumstances. His gun comes up. To make sure he won't miss, he lines up the front bead with a rear bead or with the top of the receiver. The bird is going straight away. When the gunner shoots he knows he is dead on; he thinks that if he were using a rifle he'd cut the bird in two. But he shoots his shotgun and the bird sails on. Why? In his attempt to get perfect aim, he concentrates on the sights and his gun becomes stationary. The bird is moving. Aiming has made the gunner try to hit a moving object with a stationary gun.

The actual front sight of a shotgun (forget the bead) is the forward portion of the barrel near the muzzle. What of the rear sight? Well, the height of the eye above the front sight is determined by the position of the cheek on the stock, and *that* is determined by the height of the comb. So it can be said that the comb is, in effect, the rear sight. One could even argue that the eye itself is the rear sight, and the comb simply the elevation mechanism.

A comb that is too high will make a man see too much barrel and overshoot, but this fault is not common among American factory guns. Many have combs that are a bit too low for anyone except a man with a thick face and wide cheekbones. Consequently the eye does not find its proper place in relation to the muzzle. The shooter tries to use the receiver of his gun as he would the rear sight of a rifle. He becomes an aimer — not a pointer — and a slow shot.

If a gun fits correctly, it is easy and natural for the man behind it to become a fast and good shot. If it does not fit, he tends to become an aimer and a slow, poky, mediocre shot.

The gunner does not need the pinpoint aim of the small-bore rifle shooter who is trying to stay in the 1-in. X-ring at 100 yd. Our skeet shooter or upland gunner, using approximately improved-cylinder boring and smacking his bird or his clay target at an average of 25 yd. or so, has about a 32-in. pattern to work with, and our trapshooter who breaks his clays at 35 yd. has about a 38-in. pattern to hit with if he uses a modified boring, and a 32-in. pattern with full choke.

Extreme sight consciousness or "aiming" is responsible for many faults in shooting the shotgun. It makes the gunner wait so long in getting his sights just right that the bird moves out to where the pattern is no longer effective. Aiming is also greatly responsible for the almost universal habit of slowing or stopping the swing. The shooter pays more attention to his sights than he does to his target and when they look just right he pauses, lets her go, and misses. That pause is what causes the miss.

At the other extreme, there are gifted (but unobservant) "pointers" who concentrate so much on the target they never see the muzzle at all, or so they say. Some tell me they simply see the target, throw the

48

gun up, and fire the instant the butt strikes the shoulder. They see the muzzle, all right, but they are concentrating so hard on the target they do not remember seeing it.

The fast shooter is the successful shooter; here's one getting ready for a shot. Note that he brings his head forward and down as the gun comes up. He gets his face in the right position, then puts the stock against it—not the other way round.

One day last season my dog came to a point. I walked in and flushed a cock pheasant. I shot, and while the bird was still falling I heard another get up. I whirled, saw it was a cock, shot, and dropped it. As it fell I wondered where I had held. I could not say. I must have given it the correct lead, but I can't remember.

About 90 percent of good pointing is done with the feet and the face *before* the gun is mounted. That sounds screwy, I'll admit, but let's explain.

The man who steps into his shot correctly — with his left foot advanced and a line from right to left toe angling about 45 degrees from the target flight — has won half his battle, since he is in an easy, flexible position. Those who try to shoot off the right foot or with the feet incorrectly placed almost always miss.

As the skilled shooter steps into position, he first gets his head down to the position it should be in for proper sighting and *then* brings his gun up to shoot. The good shot puts his gun to his face, and not his face to his gun.

In effect, by placing his feet and bringing his head down, he has already started to point before he gets his gun up.

As he steps into the shot, his head should be in exactly the place it will be when he fires the gun. If he is shooting well he should be able to look at an object, bring his gun up, and find it precisely aligned on the mark.

A common reason for missing — besides the pokiness of aiming — is that the hunter brings up his gun first, then starts to put his head down. But he is in a hurry. That cock pheasant looks as big as a horse and it glitters like a Christmas tree. He feels rushed. Instead of putting his head down where it belongs against the comb of the stock, he touches her off — and overshoots because he has seen too much barrel, his eye having been too high.

If a man steps into a shot, runs his neck out, and then brings his gun up, only to find he must move his head to correct his position, his gun either does not fit him or he has not trained himself to mount it correctly, getting his head down properly. And he can *never* train himself to put his head in exactly the same position each time unless the comb of the stock is right.

Most shots at pheasants are very easy and a good gunner can make longer runs on them than on any other birds I know of except decoyed ducks or doves coming in to water holes. A good man should kill 75 percent of the pheasants he shoots at, because the cock pheasant is a large and conspicuous mark that gets under way slowly. Under ordinary upland hunting conditions he is shot at relatively easy angles. It is the *hunting* of the pheasant that is fascinating, not the *shooting,* just as it is the stalking of the mountain sheep; the actual shooting of most rams is easy compared to knocking over a bounding white-tail buck in the brush.

I am a fairly good quail shot and have been shooting quail for 40 years. I do not believe I have ever killed 10 straight quail, and if I average 50 percent I think I am doing well. A quail is a small mark. He gets off the ground fast and he is tricky. The blue, Gambel's, and valley quail are dark and inconspicuous. Particularly to a man used to shooting pheasants they look like jet-propelled bumblebees.

On the other hand, I have shot more than a dozen straight pheasants without a miss, and there isn't much excuse for a good shot to miss one that gets up within range.

But they are missed. How come? Every year I find myself shooting less effectively at the end of the season than I do at the beginning. Again, how come? I have a theory that may or may not be right. In October the weather is pretty balmy. I hunt in a wool shirt and a shooting vest. Along in November it is colder. I hunt either in a shooting coat over a couple of wool shirts or in a wool shirt and a down jacket with a shooting vest over the jacket. The extra padding means that in effect I am shooting a gun with a length of pull about ¼ in. longer. Since my face is farther back on the comb, I actually shoot a gun with more drop. Now and then, particularly when a big cock catches me off base, I find that the butt catches in my jacket. When that happens my timing is destroyed. I find myself aiming and I am pretty likely to miss. Even when my gun comes up right, my face is farther back on the comb. The muzzles do not look right. I have to correct, to aim instead of point. Again my timing is loused up.

It is surprising how many shotgun shooters think they ought to shoot with their heads up. I constantly get complaints from men who have bought new guns and are unhappy because they must run their necks out in order to look down the barrel. Apparently they want to shoot in a military position with their shoulders back and their chins up. A gun stocked to permit this would be a monstrosity, slow and awkward to point and with a kick like a mule.

No one can be a good shotgunner without training himself first to get his head to the position it should be in when he shoots, and then bring his gun up. No one can become a good shot unless he trains himself to make fast alignment with the muzzle, focusing on game

51

rather than on barrel, and then shooting quickly. The more precisely he tries to aim, the longer he takes; and the longer he takes the more chance there is for him to slow or stop his swing.

Since the muzzle of the shotgun is the front sight, anything that promotes good visibility makes pointing easier and speeds up shooting. Many gunners like fairly large and conspicuous ivory beads. Others swear by gold or by red plastic. I am not conscious of seeing the bead at all, although others may be. The ventilated rib on a shotgun is one of the best of all sighting devices, since it leads the eye to the target. It's particularly good for the trapshooter, who mounts and cheeks his gun before the bird is called for, since it instantly reveals any misalignment.

Some shooters have tried wrapping the muzzle of a gun with white adhesive tape to make it conspicuous in relation to the target. The bright aluminum Cutts Comp serves exactly the same purpose, and many skeet shooters go for it. The small muzzle of a .410 is not the most conspicuous thing in the world, and many a chap has improved his small-bore skeet shooting by dressing up the muzzle. One lad I know keeps the last few inches of his .410 pump barrel coated with bright-red nail lacquer, and swears by his scheme.

Muzzle and comb — those are the things that have to be right if the shotgun is to line up right.

Any rear sight on the barrel of a shotgun is superfluous, since the actual rear sight is the correctly placed eye. The end of the barrel serves as the front sight, and pointing consists of determining the relationship of barrel and target. See that it is right, keep the gun moving, and shoot quickly. Then you'll hit.

But try to line up two beads, or use the receiver as a rear sight, and and forget your target consciousness, slow down, and miss. Everything that promotes target consciousness promotes speed and hitting. Everything that promotes sight consciousness tends to slow the gunner down, make him aim, and help him miss.

CHAPTER VI

Handguns Are Handy

**Whether for plinking, target shooting,
or small game, they'll provide sport
and sharpen the rifleman's eye**

ALONG with a shotgun, a big-game rifle, and a varmint rifle of some sort, a good handgun belongs in the battery of every man interested in firearms and shooting. A handgun is a lot of fun to plink with, and skill acquired with it is quickly translated into skill with a rifle. Because of its light weight and small bulk it can be carried when a longer and heavier weapon would be left at home.

A pal of mine does a lot of trout fishing in a canyon that is infested with rattlesnakes, and in the course of years they have bitten several anglers. So a little .22 automatic with a 4½-in. barrel is an important part of his equipment. Each season he knocks the heads off from 10 to 20 rattlers. Largely because of his efforts and those of a few other pistol-packin' fishermen, the snakes are being put under control.

I have another friend — Rollin Edmonds, principal of a junior high school in Tucson, Ariz. — who is a fine shot with any weapon and something of a handgun nut. He carries a pistol or revolver in his car at all times — just as he does a spare tire — and it has brought him many curious adventures. One night he was driving along a desert road in southern Arizona when his startled eyes beheld a big mountain lion, sharply defined in his headlights, crossing the road. Quickly he swerved the car to keep the big cat in the glare and reached into the glove compartment for — of all things! — a little .25 Colt pocket automatic. As he poked the roscoe out the window

53

the cat was standing on the shoulder of the road, apparently blinded by the headlights, and about 35 yd. away. My friend pointed the diminutive gun at the cat and squeezed off a shot. The lion jumped about 5 ft. into the air and took off.

If you practice on a range you'll find experts both ready and able to help you.

Edmonds went on into town and picked up a friend who had a couple of cold-trailing lion hounds. At dawn they were at the scene of the shooting. The dogs took the trail and found the cat as dead as a wedge about 1½ miles from where it had been shot. The bullet had penetrated both lungs and the lion had bled to death.

A few months later Edmonds was rolling along another country road in his car. It was late afternoon but visibility was good. This time he was armed with a Colt Target Woodsman loaded with .22 Long Rifle hollow-points. He saw a young mountain lion slowly walking up a hill about 100 yd. away. Edmonds stopped the car and got his sights on the cat just as it paused on the skyline. He held about level with its backbone over the lung area and squeezed off his shot. Again there was that telltale and frantic leap, and the cougar took off as if it had been scalded. Edmonds ran up the hill, hoping to get in another shot. But it was unnecessary. He found the cat dead 150 yd. from where it had been hit.

Varmint shooting with a .22 handgun can be both sporting and effective. A hollow-point bullet from one dropped this coyote.

Now, I don't contend that the .22 handgun is a weapon for big game. Edmonds was very lucky. He may prowl the country roads for the rest of his days without ever running into another lion. But luck or no luck, he never would have bagged those cats (trophies of a lifetime) if he hadn't made it a practice to carry a handgun in his car. A .22 handgun is a tool, not a toy. A trapper, for instance, can hardly afford to be without one. And Jay Bruce, the noted California lion hunter, used a .22 pistol to kill dozens, if not hundreds, of lions treed by his dogs.

It is far easier to learn to shoot a rifle passably well than it is to learn to shoot a handgun. Every shooting fault a man can display with a rifle is magnified tenfold with a handgun. The rifle's greater weight and bulk permit a little flinching and trigger yanking without making the result instantly evident. Not so with the handgun; the slightest tendency to flinch or yank the trigger is fatal to accuracy.

Many a man who does very well with the rifle finds, upon shooting a handgun, that he cannot keep his shots in a 1-ft. circle at 25 yd., and that in plinking he can't hit one bottle or can in 10. The usual reaction is a yelp that the gat is inaccurate. It's far more likely, though, that our boy is yanking the trigger. He probably does the same thing when he shoots a rifle, where it's not so noticeable, but now his sins are catching up with him.

Practice with a handgun cannot fail to help a rifleman. A good handgun shot is always a good rifle shot, particularly from the offhand position. On the other hand, many good rifle shots are only fair with a handgun, and some are pretty poor. Offhand is the most difficult of rifle positions, as far as accuracy is concerned, because it's unstable, and this same instability marks handgun shooting. In each case, shooting from the hind legs calls for relaxation and trigger control.

A great advantage of the handgun is its small weight and bulk. It can be taken along when no one would think of lugging a rifle, and the handgun owner can get a lot of informal practice on occasions where otherwise he probably wouldn't shoot at all.

Under certain conditions the handgun can be used on varmints. Years ago, big antelope jackrabbits were astonishingly plentiful in the Southwest — so plentiful and tame that shooting them with a rifle was no sport at all. I used to take a .22 revolver with me and pop away at jacks within 100-yd. range. I missed a lot beyond 50 yd., of course, but I also hit enough to keep me interested.

Just what sort of handgun should this general-purpose job be? One thing's certain — it should be a .22, for which ammunition is cheap, widely distributed, and deadly on small game. Report and recoil are light, so the .22 is the one to learn with.

The handgun can be either a revolver or an automatic pistol. Each type has its advantages. The revolver is probably safer, since you can tell at a glance whether it's loaded or not. The revolver is also more adaptable — it takes .22 shorts, longs, and Long Rifles. Then too, some people seem to take to the revolver more readily than to the pistol. Don't ask me why; it just happens. I'm one of those strange people: a revolver somehow feels better, more natural, in my hand than a pistol does.

I'm often asked if .22 shorts will seriously damage the chambers

Some .22 handguns: 1. Colt Officers' Model target revolver. 2. The Smith & Wesson K-22. Their adjustable sights make both revolvers suitable for formal and informal target shooting. 3. Harrington & Richardson Model 999, moderately priced and accurate. 4. Ruger Mark I target pistol, also inexpensive and accurate. 5. Hi-Standard Sport-King with 4½-in. barrel. 6. Colt Sport Model Woodsman with 4½-in. barrel.

of a revolver. In the days before the introduction of noncorrosive priming, all .22 weapons had a relatively short life. That's because a high concentration of rust-causing priming salts in .22 cartridges quickly started oxidation in any arm chambered for them. If a revolver were used with shorts, the forward portion of each chamber would pit; then it became difficult to seat the longer .22 Long Rifle cartridge. When the cartridge was fired, it was hard to extract the case, because its forward portion had expanded a trifle into the pits.

That particular headache hasn't existed for 25 years or so, because all .22 rimfire ammunition has been primed with various noncorrosive mixtures. Now the only hazard is erosion — eating away the steel of the chamber by hot powder gases. That's not much of a prob-

Here's good reason to have adjustable sights on a handgun—different loads may shoot quite differently. The upper group here was made with one brand of ammunition, and the lower group with another.

lem. Pressures are low in .22 ammunition. The amount of powder used is small, and burning is relatively cool. So, while theoretically the long-continued use of shorts will eventually cause pitting and make it hard to seat .22 Long Rifle cartridges, actually that contingency is very remote. I have a Smith & Wesson K-22 through which I've shot thousands of rounds of shorts, and thousands of Long Rifles as well. As far as I can tell, Long Rifle cartridges seat as easily as they ever did. And by using shorts for plinking I have probably saved enough money to buy a couple of new cylinders.

The .22 automatic pistol is a more "logical" and less complicated weapon than the revolver. Years ago I read a prediction that the automatic was going to put the revolver out of business, because the latter is more complicated, harder to manufacture, less accurate, and, in fact, a sort of dinosaur among firearms. That was a pretty bum guess; the revolver is still with us and still has its admirers, who wouldn't be caught dead shooting anything else.

The automatic pistol does have many real advantages. Most people can shoot it a bit better than the revolver. For rapid fire it has it all over the revolver; in the .22 class almost no serious target shooters try to pit revolvers against automatics. The automatic is flatter in design, less bulky, and more comfortable to carry in a holster.

But in the hands of a *careless* person, it's definitely more dangerous than the revolver, because one can't readily see if it's loaded. Neither weapon is dangerous, though, if handled with care, never pointed at anyone, and always put away unloaded.

A handgun for informal target shooting, plinking, and small-game hunting should, I believe, have a fairly short barrel. From 4 to 5 in. is about right, although many prefer long barrels. The Ruger standard model has a 4¾-in. barrel; the Smith & Wesson .22 Combat Masterpiece and the S. & W. .22/32 Kit Gun have 4-in. barrels. The Colt Sport Model Woodsman and the Challenger have 4½-in. barrels. A 6-in. barrel is not bad, though. I have used a Colt Officers' Model .22 and a Smith & Wesson K-22 for years. A pal of mine has shot hundreds of grouse and cottontails with a Harrington & Richardson Model 999, and a trapper I know has carried an Iver Johnson Model 833 Sealed 8 thousands of miles on a trapline, collecting hundreds of dollars' worth of spruce squirrels with it.

Adjustable sights are probably a good idea on the plinking handgun, since no two persons shoot any sort of weapon exactly alike. Too, the same weapon will group .22 shorts and Long Rifles differently, also standard-velocity and high-speed ammunition. However, very creditable shooting can be done with the rugged fixed sights.

Anyone who will do much small-game shooting with a .22 handgun has a lot of surprises in store. I got one of the biggest shocks of my life when I discovered that three grouse out of four fly away when hit squarely through the body with a .22 high-speed solid-point bullet. The remedy is to use hollow-points. There many be some handgun men good enough to shoot the heads off grouse at from 15 to 30 yd., but I've never seen one do his stuff.

It seems strange that with solid bullets the .22 short is apparently much more deadly on small game than is the .22 Long Rifle. I didn't believe that until I shot blue grouse for the pot now and then with a revolver. About three-fourths of those hit with Long Rifle solids flew away, and if it weren't for a very remarkable dog, I'd often have gone grouse-hungry.

A pal — a man who always carries a .22 handgun and who has killed hundreds of grouse with it — told me that I'd do better with .22 shorts. He contended that the Long Rifle solid bullet goes clear through the grouse, wasting most of its energy, but that the shorts stop inside the body and effect a kill. His own grouse pistol was a little Hi-Standard chambered for shorts. I tried it and it bore out his argument, for I killed three-fourths of the grouse I hit.

There is a lot of fun to be had with the plinking handgun, but anyone who uses it should also use some judgment. The chap who gets bored with trout fishing, and starts popping away at random in a spot where there are 15 or 20 fishermen to the mile is making enemies for all handgun users. So is the lad who picnics in a farmer's wood lot and then leaves it littered with pop bottles he has broken with his .22 handgun. It's a grand and instructive little weapon if it's treated right and not abused.

CHAPTER VII

Use the Right Bullet

**Here's why they act as they do
in their various uses**

MANY different effects are demanded of bullets for big game. To shoot smallish, thin-shelled animals like antelope at long range, what we want is a bullet that will expand readily against light resistance. Yet such a bullet, if used in shooting large animals like elk at moderates ranges, might go to pieces too quickly, particularly if it had to break large bones or penetrate much meat in order to strike a vital area. At the other extreme, there are bullets designed for the deepest possible penetration against enormous animals with massive bones and thick hides — creatures like rhinoceros, elephant, and Cape buffalo.

Back in the days of muzzle-loaders most bullets were spherical and of relatively pure lead. So all the rifleman who wanted deeper penetration could do was to use a bigger ball. The larger the animal hunted, the larger the hole had to be in the end of the barrel. In those days elephants and other dangerous game were shot with ponderous 10, 8, and even 4 bore guns with bullets that weighed 1/10, 1/8, and 1/4 lb. respectively. Curiously some people, judging a rifle's killing power by the hole in the end of the barrel, still consider a .45/70 a better elk cartridge than a .30/06, and an 8 mm. Mauser a better deer cartridge than the .270.

When smokeless powders, long bullets, and increased velocity came in, the ballisticians discovered that to function properly the lead bullets needed overcoats of some stronger and tougher metal. So they put jackets on them — "envelopes," they're called in England. Various materials were used — cupro-nickel, gilding metal, pure copper, mild steel, a layer of gilding metal over a layer of mild steel.

Early jacketed hunting bullets for soft-skinned game were all round-nose jobs like the 220-gr. .30/40 bullet and the 175-gr. 7 x 57 mm. Mauser. Most had a muzzle velocity of from 2,000 to 2,200 foot seconds. Expansion was obtained by leaving the jacket off the forward portion of the bullet to form what was called a soft nose or soft point. The more lead exposed, the quicker the expansion.

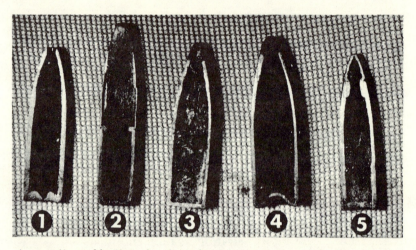

A sampling of bullets that have been cross-sectioned. 1. Open-point 172-gr. .30 caliber with gilding metal jacket. 2. German semi-spitzer soft point in 8 mm. 3. Speer soft point 180-gr. .30 caliber. 4. Ditto in 250-gr. .35 caliber. 5. Winchester 130-gr. pointed soft-point, which helped make the 270's reputation.

Bullets that are just the reverse of soft points were given to the boys who wanted deep penetration. Known to us as full-metal-cased and to the British as "solid," they have an open base and the forward portion is enclosed in metal.

For muzzle velocities of around 2,000 foot seconds both sorts were satisfactory — and still are. On light game like deer, for instance, the surest-killing 170-gr. .30/30 load is still the old-fashioned soft point with plenty of lead exposed at the tip.

Early in this century, it was discovered that a bullet with a sharp (spitzer) point had a much flatter trajectory than a round-nose job.

The Germans loaded their 7.9 x 57 mm. Model 1905 cartridge with a 154-gr. spitzer bullet at about 2,900 foot seconds. America brought out the .30/06 with a 150-gr. bullet at 2,700, and Canada introduced the .280 Ross with a 145-gr. bullet at 3,060. Then came the .22 Savage Hi-Power with a 70-gr. bullet at 2,800 and the .250/3000 Savage with an 87-gr. bullet at 3,000. The late Charles Newton, who designed these last two loads, also introduced a whole flock of hot-shot big-game calibers from .256 to .35 with velocities of around 3,000.

Right away the boys started having bullet troubles. Those early high-velocity spitzers had soft points of the same soft lead core, and with the same thin jacket, as the old round-nose bullets that were shot at around 2,000 foot seconds. Quickly the hunters started hollering. The points battered in the magazine until they looked like miniature mushrooms, the users declared, and instead of penetrating into an animal's boiler room they often flew to pieces on the surface.

Lads who slave for the ammunition factories started tackling bullet design in a serious way almost 50 years ago, and they're still at it. Their task is complicated by the fact that the average rifle user wants an all-round bullet, and there ain't no such animal and never will be. Let's see why.

The sharp point zips through the air fast, and without losing much velocity, but is easily deflected by brush. What's more, it is the poorest possible form to build an expanding device into. Contrariwise, the round nose, which gets through brush well and which is easy to make expand, sheds velocity in great hunks and therefore isn't so hot for long-range shooting.

Yet the boys want a bullet that will retain its velocity with maximum efficiency, shoot as accurately as a match bullet, get through brush, and expand properly on a white-tail deer weighing from 125 to 165 lb. on the hoof or on a moose weighing maybe 1,500 lb. No wonder the designers climb trees!

In well over 30 years as a practicing gun nut, I've watched the pendulum swing back and forth. A certain bullet comes out and the customers scream that it goes to pieces like smoke. The factory makes another and they complain that it goes right through game without expansion.

Let's see what can be done to control bullet performance upon impact — for rapid expansion, or for deep penetration, as the case may be.

Expansion on game is dependent on many things: 1. Velocity at time of impact. The faster a bullet is traveling when it hits, the more violently it expands. A bullet that may expand satisfactorily at 100 yd. may drive clear through game at 300. . . . 2. Jacket thickness, particularly toward the point. . . . 3. The hardness and toughness of the jacket. . . . 4. The hardness of the lead core. I knew a small bullet-maker who tried to cut costs by reclaiming shot from a trap layout. The lead was far too hard. Next season most of his customers reported shooting through bucks from stem to stern without much result. . . . 5. The amount of lead exposed at the tip. . . . 6. Reinforcement of jacket with fold, belt, solid base, etc. . . . 7. Weakening of jacket with cannelures (American practice) or splits (British practice). . . . 8. Character of device at forward end to promote expansion — hollow point, capped soft point, wedge, etc.

At one extreme we have a bullet with a soft core of pure lead covered with a soft, thin jacket. For a time I used a 120-gr. .270 spitzer soft point of that sort, loaded to about 3,200 foot seconds, on jackrabbits, coyotes, javelinas, and little Southwestern white-tail deer weighing about 100 lb. field-dressed. The bullet would go completely to pieces in the chest of the deer. No portion would go through, and the whole chest cavity would be a mush filled with bits of lead and tiny hunks of jacket. On light game shot broadside the bullet killed instantly, yet it would be worthless for heavier game.

At the other extreme we have a full-metal-case round-nose bullet weighing around 500 gr., designed for maximum penetration on the biggest game — a bullet that will break both shoulders of a rhino or drive through an elephant's skull into the brain. Such a bullet has a hard lead core and heavy walls, and its business end is of heavy reinforced steel — yes, steel — almost flat in contour.

Best *compromise* bullet is so constructed that its forward portion will open up at relatively low velocity at long range against light resistance, yet hold together at the high velocity of short range against heavy resistance. Examples include the Silvertip, with its reinforced multiple jacket and soft point protected by metal, and the Core-Lokt with the jacket locked around the core.

Results with even the best bullets vary On a given sort of animal, one hunter will claim that a certain bullet goes to pieces too quickly, while another hunter will insist that the damned bullet doesn't open up at all. Bullet effect is governed not only by the construction but by the impact velocity. (It makes a lot of difference whether you shoot an animal at 50 yd. or at 400.) It also matters where you hit — in the rump (relatively soft muscles), rib cage (relatively thin bone and cartilage), shoulder (relatively heavy bone), or stomach (thin layer of skin over moisture-filled bag).

Pal of mine named Jack Holliday, when we were hunting in Alberta in 1943, took a pop at a grizzly with a .22/.250 with a 41-gr. Sisk bullet loaded to a muzzle velocity of about 4,200 foot seconds. First bullet cracked the massive shoulder blade but flew to pieces. Second bullet struck between ribs and blew up in one lung. The grizzly fell in its tracks. Conclusion from the first bullet would be that the .22/.250 is no good on grizzly, and from the second bullet that it's poison!

The picture is further complicated by occasional freak performance which evidently comes from a defective bullet. With a certain 150-gr. .30 caliber bullet I once shot a heavy ram at about 75 yd. as it ran directly away from me. The bullet struck in the ham, went through abdomen and lungs, and out through the brisket, making an exit hole but little larger than where it went in. With another such bullet I shot a mule deer broadside through the rib cage at about the same range. Bullet blew up on a rib, killed the deer with the debris, but made a hole the size of a saucer where it went in. How come?

Bullets get the blame for a lot of lousy shooting, by the way. Guy I knew came to me about 10 years ago and asked me what to use on an antelope hunt. I had just returned from a successful one, told him I had used a .270 with the 130-gr. Winchester pointed-expanding bullet. He came back empty-handed and with his nose out of joint, to report that he'd hit an antelope four times right in the lungs at 100 yd. or so and that the pronghorn just kept going. The bullets, he said, hadn't opened up at all. I cross-questioned the guy. Had he seen blood? No. Had he seen hair fly? No. Did the antelope stumble, go down, or otherwise show it was hit? No. I could only conclude that he had simply missed four times and was blaming the bullet.

For light, fragile game like antelope and small deer, what's wanted isn't deep penetration but quick expansion. Around 15 years ago I took a .257 on a month's hunting trip into Mexico. Bullets I used had very thick jackets and small open points with shallow cavities. I had a heck of a time with them, for the deer I hit would run merrily on and had to be whittled down. One buck was shot precisely through the heart, and there was no sign of expansion at all. The only deer I killed cleanly was one that was standing behind a tree. The bullet went through the tree and was pretty well expanded by the time it hit the deer. Since it was hardly feasible to carry a tree around to shoot at deer through, I came back pretty sour on that bullet.

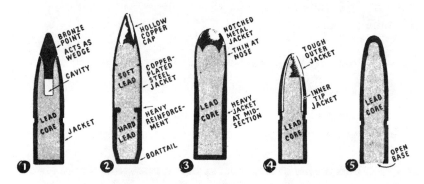

Diagrams of various bullet types. 1. Remington Bronze Point. 2. R.W.S. 173-gr. 7x64 mm. Torpedo-jacket boattail, one of the fanciest bullets ever made. 3. Remington Core-Lockt. 4. Winchester-Western Silvertip. 5. Full-metal-case bullet.

But there are times when you *want* penetration; and sectional density of a bullet (weight in pounds divided by area of cross section, as expressed in inches) is an important factor in obtaining it. The relatively light 160-gr. 6.5 mm. Mannlicher-Schoenauer soft point has been successful on lions, and the full-metal-case version has even been used for head shots on elephants. Likewise the 175-gr. bullet for the 7x57. Neither bullet was particularly heavily constructed, yet being long and skinny it had great sectional density and gave the desired results.

In obtaining deep penetration, construction can replace sectional density to some extent. Example is the 180-gr. Remington pointed soft-point Core-Lokt, which will go through grizzly, elk, or caribou like a chorus girl through a C-note. With it I've shot two grizzlies and three big bull caribou. I've yet to recover one of those bullets; they

66

all went clear through to blast rocks or down timber on the animal's far side. In two cases the bullets broke shoulders of grizzlies while they were about it and in one case broke the off shoulder of a caribou.

Most experienced guides recommend the 220-gr. bullet in .30 caliber rifles for Alaska brown bear (if indeed they don't demand that the hunter fetch along a .375 Magnum). But my pal Herb Klein called me up from Dallas a while back to tell me about killing a brownie with the 180-gr. Nosler bullet driven at very high velocity in his .300 Weatherby Magnum. Bullet struck the bruin behind one shoulder, broke the one on the far side, left about a .40 caliber exit hole, and sailed on across Bering Strait into Siberia.

Only a lousy little 180-gr. bullet on North America's largest and most dangerous bear, yet if *because of its construction* it does not have ample penetration, then my name is Molotov.

Once Roy Weatherby sent me a .257 Weatherby Magnum to try out. I had some 117-gr. full-metal-case .25/35 bullets around, so I loaded them up to a muzzle velocity of probably around 3,100 foot seconds and took the rifle out on a jackrabbit hunt. You might think a full-jacketed bullet of this sort would not expand at all. But don't forget the joker. That bullet was designed to leave the muzzle at around 2,200 foot seconds. Jacket was thin, core was soft. At over 3,000 foot seconds it exploded jacks like a bomb. I blundered into a coyote, leveled down on him, and blew his far side off!

Just because a bullet is full-jacketed is no sign that it will hold together. Many a hunter in Africa has found that ordinary "solid" bullets will break up on the heavy skull or shoulder bone of rhino, buffalo, and elephant. The very heaviest type of jacket is called for here, so the bullet will not only hold together but keep its shape and drive through to the vitals.

Preserving the spitzer shape of a bullet, yet constructing it so that it will expand, is a tough assignment which has been met in various ways.

A cheap and simple method is merely to swage jacket and bullet to spitzer shape, controlling expansion by the amount of lead exposed at the point, the hardness of the lead, and jacket thickness toward the point. One catch here, though, is that recoil batters and flattens the points of unused bullets in the magazine. Furthermore, the bullet often upsets or becomes foreshortened in the bore, so when it leaves the muzzle it does not have the beautiful spitzer shape it began with. What happens is that the impact of the gases against the base of the bullet starts the base moving before the front, and the phenomenon is called "slugging in the bore."

Another stunt is to use an open point, controlling expansion by the diameter and depth of the cavity, thickness of metal toward the point, and hardness of the core. Particularly for quick expansion, the open point is excellent, and no bullet ever manufactured has had more friends than the famous 180-gr. Western open point for the .30/06. Rub is, though, that no open point can have a true spitzer shape.

The Remington Bronze Point obtains true spitzer shape and fine ranging qualities by the use of a bronze wedge over a cavity. When the point hits, the wedge drives back, splitting the jacket and letting the cavity get in its work. I like the bullet very much. The 150-gr. .30/06 is my favorite deer medicine. The 130-gr. .270 is a very fine bullet too. Expansion is good but not too violent and I have never had any trouble in getting sufficient penetration. With it I shot a very big moose three times through the lungs, and found all the funny little bronze points stuck in the hide on the far side.

In 1949, using the 180-gr. Bronze Point loaded to about 3,200 foot seconds in a .300 Weatherby Magnum, I shot a grizzly at about 125 yd. He pitched over on his nose and that was that. Hole behind far shoulder was size of a saucer and there was a fan-shaped spray of blood, rib fragments, and bits of lung 3 ft. long and 3 ft. wide. With that combination the hunter can go after grizzly with very little risk.

Western-Winchester preserves semi-spitzer shape with the Silvertip by protecting the soft lead point by a thin jacket of tin. Same stunt was used on the Winchester protected soft-point bullets in .25, .270, and .30 caliber. They are now obsolete, but the 130-gr. .270 bullet of that construction, with its sharp point and heavy reinforced base, was largely responsible for making the reputation of the .270 cartridge. It was an expensive bullet to manufacture — but so are Bronze Points and Silvertips.

The Germans made many very fine and elaborate bullets and have greatly influenced American bullet design. One of the most intricate is the famous R.W.S. Torpedo-jacket bullet made by the Rheinisch-Westfalische Sprengstoff Aktien Gesellschaft in Nuremberg. No. 2

in the sketch shows one in cross section — a 173-gr. job for the 7 x 64. I showed that bullet to a manufacturer. He turned pale and said, "Great Scott! If I made those I'd have to peddle them for two bits apiece."

It begins to look as if this bullet business is a bit complicated, then, and that instead of just walking in and demanding some .30/06 fodder, the customer should do a little thinking about what results he wants and on what!

CHAPTER VIII

Load Your
Own Ammunition

Handloading can save you money and
give your gun new possibilities

O NCE, some years ago, after I'd written something about handloading a big-game cartridge, a hunter took pen in hand to ask
if I'd actually be foolish enough to go on a big-game hunt with handloaded ammunition. He could see some percentage in handloading
reduced loads for practice and for small game, he wrote. But full-
power loads? Uh, uh!

My answer to that query was, why not? What the factories put in
the hind end of a case is a primer, and what they put in the front
end is a bullet. What they put inside the case is powder. The careful
handloader who knows what it's all about can do the same thing. His
home-brewed ammunition will make just as much noise, kick just as
hard, and kill just as dead.

But let me make an important point: The handloader undertakes
to reload his cartridges on his own responsibility. Therefore he must
be a careful, cautious man. If, through ignorance or carelessness, he
overloads a case, the result may be a blown-up rifle and serious personal injury. So if you're a woolgatherer, or are inclined to take
chances, fool around with some other hobby.

On the range where I practice, another shooter, whom I call the
Mysterious Mr. X, also burns up ammunition. Mr. X evidently likes
to shoot, and apparently he wants to be a big-game shot. I have never

seen him. He may be young or old, tall or short, handsome or homely. I do know, though, that he is (a) rich or (b) crazy or (c) innocent. His quota for a practice session — two boxes of factory ammunition — costs him about $8. He leaves the firing point strewn with

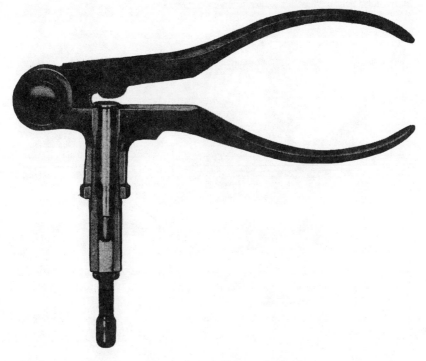

This tong tool is particularly useful to the rifleman who does a little reloading and can take his time. Its fittings eject the old primer, resize the case, expand the neck and seat the bullet (above) in separate operations.

glittering Winchester .30/06 cases. Furtively I gather them up — if someone does not beat me to them. I take them home, run them through a full-length resizing die so they can be used in any .30/06 rifle. Then I put in a new primer, the proper powder charge, and another bullet.

Mr. X's practice costs him about 20 cents a shot, five shots for a dollar. Let's see what mine costs. Primers bought at retail set me back about three-quarters of a cent apiece; the powder charge — depending on what and how much I use, anywhere from half a cent to around 1½ cents. Jacketed bullets cost around 4½ cents each. I wind

71

up with a perfectly satisfactory, accurate, full-power load at an average cost of less than 7 cents. Moreover, I have just the load I want — perhaps for a jackrabbit, perhaps for a moose. Mr. X's 40-shot practice session costs him about $8, a sum which will, even in these days, buy

The Handloader's materials (l. to r.): The cartridge case, bullet, powder, and primer.

numerous bottles of sarsaparilla pop, a large roast, or a pair of shoes for baby. My practice isn't exactly for free, but at least it's a luxury a wage earner can allow himself now and then.

The gimmick in all this is that Mr. X, in his nonchalant manner, has tossed away the most valuable part of the cartridge for which he laid down one-fifth of a dollar — the case. And when he gave it the heave-ho, it was for all intents and purposes as good as new, good for from 10 to 40 reloadings, depending on how the reloader treats it and loads it.

It has been said that to be a first-rate rifleman, one must shoot 1,000 shots a year. That may or may not be true. But if it is, let us take a look at costs. Our 1,000-shot-a-year man will spend $200 on his hobby, but a handloader can do the same amount of shooting for $70.

While our handloader saves money, he is, curiously enough, the best customer the ammunition factories have, for he actually buys more ammunition than the non-reloader. That toll of 20 cents a shot will hold the average man down to two or three boxes of ammunition a year. Our reloader will probably buy at least twice that many just for the cases. Not long ago I had a new 7 mm. Mauser rifle made up. My first purchase was five boxes of factory ammunition for it, giving me 100·cases to play with.

So it works out that the handloader does much more shooting for the same money. Because he shoots, he stimulates others to shoot. He is a man to be encouraged, cherished, and protected, to be wooed with pretty ads and fattened with handloading components.

He makes his rifle more versatile and, in many cases, more effective for a special purpose than it would be with commercial ammunition. Factories necessarily have to standardize on a relatively small number of loads. Big-game ammunition is ordinarily loaded to maximum velocity and pressure. Most calibers have a limited number of bullet weights, some only one. In others, a potentially excellent cartridge is deliberately underloaded because there are old rifles still being used that would be unsafe with a hotter load.

Take the excellent little 7 mm. Mauser cartridge. Today it is loaded only with a 175-gr. bullet. Muzzle velocity is about 2,450 foot seconds, and pressure about 47,000 pounds per square inch. A 7 mm. Model 70 Winchester will take over 50,000 lb. without whimpering and so will a good Mauser action. Not only does a case stand this somewhat higher pressure, but it can be loaded with a great variety of bullets for different purposes. As it stands, the 7 mm.'s 175-gr. soft-point bullet is a pretty good load for deer in timber, and also for elk. But its trajectory is much too curved for antelope or deer in open country at long range. The 7 mm. handloader, though, can have himself a classy antelope rifle by loading the 130-gr. Speer bullet to around 3,050 foot seconds, or the various 140-gr. bullets to around 2,850. The value of a 7 mm., then, is just about doubled by handloading.

Another example of how rifle efficiency can be greatly increased by handloading lies in the .257. Factory fodder produces about 2,900 foot seconds in the 100-gr. bullet, and less than 2,800 in the 117-gr. The factory-loaded .257 is a sort of super .250/3000. Let our handloader get hold of a .257, though, and he can feed it with the long, mean 125-gr. Barnes bullet with enough No. 4350 powder to drive it along at close to 2,900. Or he can send the 120-gr. Speer or A.B.C.

bullet slithering out of the muzzle at not much less than 3,000. Then our lad has a vicious understudy of the great .270.

Speaking of the .270, those who want to push its 130-gr. bullet faster are doomed to disappointment; that .270 load has been a race horse from the very beginning, loaded to maximum velocity and

When O'Connor depresses the lever on this bench-type tool he seats a primer and expands the case neck to just the right size to hold a bullet securely.

maximum pressure. The 150-gr. job is another story. Factories load it down to only 2,770 foot seconds, for deer hunting in the woods, making a truck horse out of a greyhound. But handload it with 53.5 or 54 gr. of No. 4350 and a long, mean, sharp-point Speer, Sierra, or

A.B.C. bullet and you boost the velocity 200 foot seconds or thereabouts, getting a fine, flat-shooting, long-range load for big game like elk. Such a bullet has the same velocity as that of the factory 150-gr. .30/06 load, and it also has considerably better sectional density and drag coefficient.

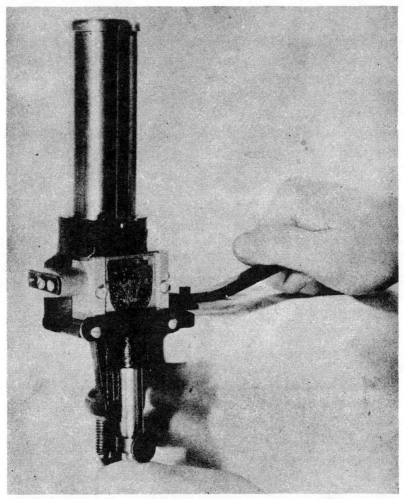

This powder measure can be set to drop exactly the right amount of powder into a case, thus speeding up the reloading.

It would be possible to go on with this list for a long time, since velocity of many cartridges can be stepped up by handloading. The handloader can get cheaper ammunition. In many cases he can get more powerful big-game loads. He can use special bullets in weights not loaded by the big companies — 120, 145, and 160-gr. bullets in the 7 mm.; 110, 120, and 160-gr. bullets in the .270; 200 and 250-gr. bullets in the .30/06 and .300 Magnum. He can load down his big-game rifle for use on small game like grouse and rabbits, and he can use light, thin-jacketed bullets at very high velocity on varmints, thus keeping his eye sharpened up for big game. During the many years I lived in Arizona I did most of my shooting on jackrabbits — antelope and black-tail — with handloaded light, fast bullets in .30/-06, .270, and .257 rifles.

Just what does this mysterious process of handloading consist of? Nothing but the replacement of components that have been used up in firing. To reload a fired cartridge case for use in the same rifle, one punches out the fired primer and inserts a new one. Then one reshapes the neck of the case so it will hold a new bullet friction-tight. This is done by sizing the neck down and then expanding it to the correct dimensions.

If the case has been originally fired in another rifle of the same caliber, it is usually necessary to resize the case full length by running it into a die made for the purpose. That brings the case back to its original factory dimensions, and it can be fired in any correctly chambered rifle of that caliber. If the case has been fired several times in a rifle that develops high pressure, it is usually wise to trim the case neck.

The next step in reloading is to put the proper amount of the correct powder into the case. Then a bullet is seated. Bingo! We are now in possession of a cartridge that is as good as one just out of the factory loading machine.

What will adequate tools cost? That depends!

My first venture into handloading was on a shoestring. I bought an Ideal tong tool (jovially called "the nutcracker") for the .30/06. Because I could afford neither a scale nor a powder measure, I made a dip measure from a filed-off cartridge case and used baling wire for a handle. I filed down the case so that when it was filled level full it held, if I remember correctly, 14 gr. of the now obsolete du Pont No. 80 powder. I loaded this behind some salvaged 150-gr. jacketed military bullets dating from the first World War — and I was in the reloading business.

Gradually I enlarged the operation. I bought bullet molds to cast lead bullets, also a resizer and lubricator that enabled me to turn out, at small cost, home-made lubricated gas-check bullets that could be driven fairly fast with good accuracy. When I ventured into full-power loads I acquired a scale to weigh each charge. I next got hold of a powder measure. Now I have scales, powder measure, cast trimmer, lubricator and sizer, case gauges, a bench-type tool with dies for the .22/.250, .220 Swift, .219 Improved Zipper, .250/3000, .257, 7 mm. Weatherby Magnum, 7 x 57, .270, .30/06, .300 Magnum, and .38 Special. With my first outfit I turned out shootable ammunition at an outlay of less than $10. This cost, however, no longer means anything.

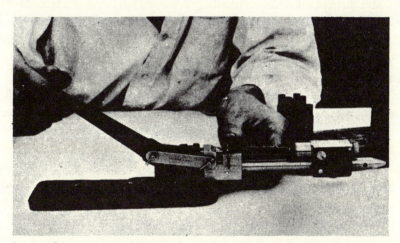

A portable tool is less expensive than the straight-line bench types but it's also slower in operation.

The Lyman tong tool is small, handy, and inexpensive, and with it one does not need a bench or other elaborate set-up. Furthermore, the ammunition loaded with it is just as good as that turned out with any other tool. It's a good bet for the man who's cramped for space and who doesn't do much reloading. But, sad to say, it's as slow as the seven-year itch. Each operation must be performed separately: decapping (removing the fired primer); neck sizing; neck expanding; and recapping (seating the new primer). After that the powder is put in the case and the bullet seated.

The heavy bench-type straight-line tools are enormously faster, preparing a case for powder and bullet in one-fourth the time. But they must be affixed to heavy benches — and even if the loader makes his own it costs money and takes up space.

Bench-type tools have the power to full-length-resize with a full-length die; the tong tool does not. The bench tools are the best bet for the man who loads a great deal of ammunition for several different calibers, since they can be adapted, with suitable case holders and dies, to everything from the .22 Hornet to the .375 Magnum.

With a tool of the Pacific type, the loader screws in and adjusts the sizing die, then puts in a case holder of the proper type. He next inserts a fired case and lifts a handle. The upstroke expels the fired primer and sizes the neck. He then puts the primer on the priming arm and brings down the handle. This second stroke expands the neck and seats the primer. His case is now ready for powder and bullet.

After the prospective handloader has chosen his tool, he must have some means of measuring powder, so his next purchase should be a scale. With it he can accurately measure each charge before he puts it into a case. Since this is slow work, he should next buy a powder measure, which can be adjusted to throw various charges. He can check his measure against the scale to see that the charge is accurate.

Gradually the handloader will add to his equipment. He'll buy case gauges, primer-pocket reamers, case trimmers. He may even decide to make his own jacketed bullets with a set of dies. He'll do a lot more shooting than he ordinarily would, and if he charges off his equipment at a fraction of a cent for each fired cartridge he will, in time, have it for free.

It is a grand hobby, this handloading, as well as a money saver, and anyone who wants to have plenty of practice with his big-game rifle should look into it. So should every varmint hunter, any big-bore target shot — in fact, everyone who likes to shoot.

CHAPTER IX

How to Sight In Your Rifle

All you need is cartridges, a few targets,
and a safe spot — Use a bedroll if no
benchrest is available

1. First step for Dr. Glen Carlson, of Lewiston, Idaho, is to set
up a 100-yard small-bore target with 6-inch bull.

2. Carlson loads his new .30/06, built on a Springfield action, with 180-grain Remington Core-Lokt ammunition. He made the gunstock himself. As for the scope, he decided on a Weaver K-25 and had it installed on a Redfield Jr. mount.

3. Target is a measured 25 yards away, against a hillside that serves as a backstop. Using a bedroll rest, Carlson touches off three shots. He calls two good, and one high.

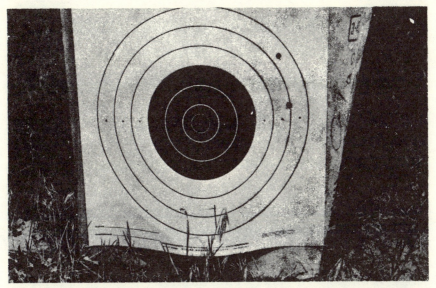

4. One shot is high, but the two others are in one hole 5 inches from the center of the target. This is the normal point of impact. Now to correct that 5-inch error.

5. Carlson reasons: "At 25 yards' range, a minute of angle has a value of ¼ inch. Each click on my scope is equal to 2 minutes of angle—or, in this case, to ½ inch. I would have to use 10 clicks, therefore, to correct a 5-inch error. That might get the reticle out of the center of the field."

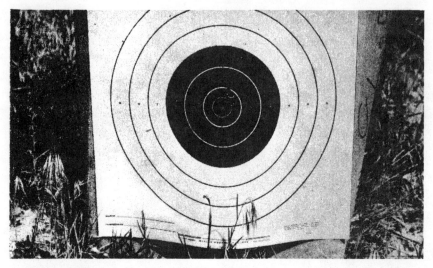

6. Instead, he makes the correction by adjusting windage screws in the scope's mount. He turns the left screw out one turn, the right one in (clockwise) until it stops. His next three shots go into the 10 ring (above). To make doubly sure, he shoots two more groups with similar results.

7. His next move is to shoot a group at 100 yards, from the sit and without a sling—as he would in deer hunting. At 100 yards, he wants his bullets to group about 3 inches high; then they will cross line of sight again at 225 yards. That way, he can ignore trajectory on ranges up to 250 yards.

8. His string of four shots at 100 yards is about 3 inches high and a shade to the right—so little it would make no difference in the field. Carlson now has accurate sighting for deer up to 250 yards, and even greater leeway on the larger game he plans to hunt. Bring on your elk and moose.

CHAPTER X

Which Sight for You?

The open sight standard on most factory
rifles is rugged, but how good is it?

EVERY once in a while some rifle fan goes into a huddle with himself and when he comes out of it he announces that the open
sight has great advantages. It is, he says, cheap, simple, light, durable,
and practically impervious to the weather. Then someone else tells
the world that the open sight is obsolete, a snare and a delusion, and
only half a cut better than no sight at all.

Actually, the open sight is hardly obsolete, since it is still being
manufactured and is still preferred by many riflemen. I think it's safe
to bet that there are more open sights in circulation than any other
type, and it's also safe to bet that more deer are killed with open-
sighted rifles than with any other kind. Probably half of all deer rifles
wear open sights, the other half peep sights and scopes.

I know of many people who want to remove good peep sights from
rifles and install open sights. And this seems to indicate that the
market for good aperture sights is a long way from saturated, and that
the one for scopes should be in a healthy state for a long, long time
— as long as the ultimate consumer has a few nickels left in his
pocket.

I'll grant that the open sight is cheap, light, and simple, and that it
doesn't become clogged with snow, twigs, and what not. I will not
concede, however, that cheapness, lightness, and simplicity are necessarily virtues in themselves.

The open sight retains its popularity largely for two reasons. It is cheap to make; consequently manufacturers put it on rifles in order to sell the things with some kind of sight. They take it for granted that some of their customers want to shoot their purchases as they come out of the carton, and that those who don't can go out and buy exactly what they want. That strikes me as good practice.

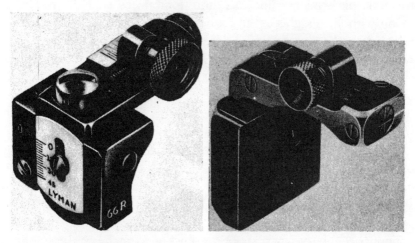

Lyman 66-R, (left) designed for the Remington Model 760 rifle, is adjustable in minutes of angle, each minute changing point of impact 1 in. in 100 yd. range. The Williams Foolproof (right) is a fine, simply constructed peep sight.

Putting a good receiver sight on a rifle would increase the retail price around $5 or $10, and anyone with merchandising experience knows that every dollar slapped onto the retail price cuts down the potential market. Further, the man who wants to use a top-mounted scope shouldn't be made to pay for a receiver sight that he'd have to discard. With few exceptions, then, factory rifles come out of the store with open sights, and a pretty high percentage are left that way — in many cases through ignorance, indifference, sloth, and inertia, but in some cases by preference.

Sad to say, the open sight is a pretty poor gimmick with which to aim. I don't say that excellent shooting has not been done with it. But the man who shoots well with it does so in spite of the sight, not because of it.

The open sight is optically all wrong. The human eye has considerable depth of focus, but not enough to focus simultaneously on a rear sight about 15 in. away, a front sight from 30 to 36 in. away, and a target from 50 to 400 yd. away. The young man with good eyes can make a stab at it, but the middle-aged man, whose eyes are, like a $2 camera, more or less in a state of "fixed focus," can no more do it than he can scratch the back of his head with his foot. About the time his arms become too short for him to read the restaurant menu without his glasses, and when the oculist shakes his head and tells him he has reached the bifocal age, he has to go to a peep sight whether he likes the idea or not. In extreme cases of farsightedness, even the front sight will look fuzzy against the target, and then the only remedy is a scope, which, happily, can be focused for his trick eyesight and which will put the game and the aiming reticle in the same optical plane.

The simpler the open sight is, the better. And optically the best type of open sight is the one with the shallow V or U and no projections or "ears." The most accurate type of open sight is the square-cut Partridge type, but it is slower than the sight with the shallow cut.

The worst problem with an open sight is maintaining correct elevation, particularly when shooting quickly, as many of the semifolklore terms of rifle shooting go to prove. "I took a *fine* bead," the deer hunter says. "I saw the goat was a long way off, so I took a real coarse bead," says the mountain hunter. "The deer jumped and I didn't take a fine enough bead and overshot him," says the lad who didn't bring home the bacon.

The narrower the cut in the V, the more difficult it is to achieve the correct elevation, since the farther down one goes into the V in trying to see the front sight, the poorer the light becomes. On a hasty shot the user of open sights won't pull down "fine" into the notch and hence will overshoot. That's because he cannot see the front sight in the bottom of the V. It is the open sight that's responsible for the ancient adage: "Always hold low on a deer."

The very best open sights blot out half the target, the poorest (including the full buckhorn with its big ears) from two-thirds to three-fourths. It is human nature to want to see what you're shooting at, so the tendency for the excited hunter is to see more deer and less rear sight — and thus overshoot. Some of the things done by excited hunters using open sights are almost beyond belief. Not long ago I was talking with a man who has done a lot of big-game hunting but apparently is a pretty sad shot. He told me how he scorned the scope because he'd always found "the good old-fashioned open sight" enough for him, and in the next breath he told how he missed a bull elk at 25 yd. What he probably did was put the front bead on the elk's neck, ignore the rear sight, and cut loose!

The Dem-Bart is interchangeable with a scope on Redfield Jr., Buehler mounts.

Another little item that causes experienced riflemen to view the ordinary open sight with scant love is the fact that it's very difficult to adjust. Most such sights simply have steps on a slide to provide for elevation. Some steps will change point of impact as little as 4 in. at 100 yd. Others as much as 1 ft. Trying to sight in precisely with such an adjustment is as fruitless as for a surgeon to tackle a delicate brain operation with an ax. If a man wants to sight in a rifle so accurately that he can, if he has to, break a buck's neck at 100 yd., he will save money by buying a receiver sight adjustable for minutes of angle. He can then sight in exactly with from 5 to 10 shots, whereas with many open sights the only thing he can do for exact adjustment is to file down a notch.

Even with a scope sight, one man cannot do a 100 percent job of sighting in for another, since Mr. A may habitually cant his rifle a bit or hold it loosely, whereas Mr. B keeps it straight and holds it firmly against his shoulder. Sighting in for someone else is even less successful with a peep sight, and with an open sight it is simply no go. One man may take a fine bead, the other a coarse bead, and so on. It is not uncommon for two cracks shots to shoot groups 2 ft. apart at 200 yd. with the same rifle and the same setting of open sights. The fact that many deer are killed annually with rifles sighted in at the factory and never checked by their owners simply shows that deer are large marks and are usually shot at close range.

Still another reason why an easily adjustable sight is desirable: The point of impact in most hunting rifles varies greatly with different weights of bullets and even with different makes and lots of ammunition using bullets of the same weight.

The aperture or peep sight is something else again — a fast, accurate sight which is optically excellent and which, in its better forms, adjusts easily and exactly. In using the peep correctly, the rifleman pays no attention to it at all, is hardly conscious of it. He simply looks *through* it, puts the front sight on what he wants to hit, and touches her off. With it there is no tendency to shoot high. The peep does not blot out any deer, and the front sight stands up plain and easy to see.

When the open-sight user first undertakes to shoot with a peep, he almost always makes the same mistakes. He worries because he can see so much through it. So he screws in a target disk, which cuts out light and slows him up. He tries hard to center his bead right in the middle of the aperture. He may even leave the open sight on the barrel and try to use both it and the peep at the same time. When that is done all value of the peep is lost. Then the shooter is simply looking through a peep to aim with an open sight.

Now the eye, naturally and without conscious effort, centers the front bead at the point of strongest light, which is the middle of the aperture. So the shooter should never bother his little curly head about it. Furthermore, the big hunting apertures are just about as accurate as the fine ones in the small target disks. I've proved that to my own satisfaction many times by testing both on the same rifle. But the small aperture is preferable for target work because it sharpens up the front sight and the target by increasing depth of focus, like a small aperture in a camera.

88

The first peep sight I ever used was one on the slide of the old Model 1903 Springfield rear sight. It was too small, too far from the eye, and worthless for anything but slow-fire target shooting. In my innocence I considered it pretty good. Then I bought a Lyman 48. I could see the whole world through it and it was easy to use, so I was sure it was no good. I screwed in a target disk that was hard to

An extension brings the sight on this target rifle closer to the eye to provide greater sighting radius.

look through and then I was happy. Late one afternoon I saw a nice buck standing on the edge of dark timber. With the naked eye I could see him nicely. Through the miserable little hole in the disk I couldn't see buck or front sight at all. When, after several seconds of peering and muttering, I took the rifle down from my shoulder and began to screw out the disk, the buck remembered a previous appointment and took off. In hunting, the thing to do is to remove the screw-in disk and bury it. Except for target shooting it is a hindrance, not a help.

For speed, the closer your eye is to the peep the better off you are, because you are going to see more through the aperture, just as the closer your eye is to a keyhole the more you can see through it. The original Lyman peep sights were mounted on the tang, but when the bolt-action rifle became so popular the tang sight was no longer practical. Most peeps are now mounted on the receiver. Examples are the famous Lyman 48 and 57, the Redfield 70 series, and the Williams "Foolproof" sights.

For fast woods shooting with a pump, automatic, or lever-action rifle of moderate recoil, I prefer a tang sight.

Tang peeps are fine hunting sights. They have the longest possible sighting radius, and because they're close to the eye one has a vast field of view. They are very fast. However, they're less easy to adjust, not quite so exact, and somewhat more fragile than receiver sights, since the long stem sits up there unprotected.

Nowadays, with the wide and growing popularity of scope sights, an iron sight is often used as an auxiliary to have on hand in case

Men who use a scope sight often carry an auxiliary peep sight of the slide-in type as insurance against the scope's being disabled by accident or bad weather.

something goes wrong with the scope. Many bridgetype scope mounts can be fitted with little peeps such as those put out by various concerns for the Redfield and Buehler mounts. Some require special high front sights; some do not.

Possibly the best stunt, if a rifleman wants an auxiliary sight, is to mount the scope on a quick-detachable side mount like the Echo, Pachmayr, Griffin & Howe, Jaeger, or Mykrom. Then as insurance against disaster the factory rear sight can be retained. The sweetest outfit of all, though, is a side-mounted scope in conjunction with a receiver sight having a quickly removable slide. I have two rifles so equipped for hunting in the north, where rain, snow, and wet buckbrush and fir at timberline may put a scope out of action. One is a .270, the other a .30/06. Both have Griffin & Howe side mounts and

Lyman 48 receiver sights. The scope can be slipped off in a matter of seconds and the slide of the 48 slipped in. When the scope is in place, the slide of the receiver sight can be carried in the pocket, but the ideal spot for it is in the recess of a trap buttplate. My .270 is equipped with one made by Emil J. Koshollek, of Stevens Point, Wis. Prior to the war many such buttplates were imported from Germany and used on fine sporters.

The open sight is simple, cheap, and easy to use, but awfully easy to miss with, especially on long shots.

For the last 25 years or more, the fashion has been to mount the front sight on a ramp base. Many factory rifles have such bases forged with the barrel in the course of manufacture. Other ramps are screwed and sweated on. Some are put on with bands. Such ramps look good, and they protect the front sight itself.

Probably the best material for the front sight is a copper alloy called "gold." Ivory beads show well under certain conditions, but I never had one that I didn't manage to knock off in short order. Red plastic, like ivory, also shows up well on occasion, but like ivory it is fragile. "Gold" shows up better under more different conditions than any other front-sight material and is also the strongest. For target use it can be blackened with the sooty flame of a kitchen match.

The conventional front sight is a bead; for all-round use one of about 3/32-in. diameter is correct. A square blade tipped with gold is a fine all-round front sight for hunting and target use, and the Sourdough made by Redfield is the most advanced of the blade-type front sights, since it is perfectly flat and square in silhouette, yet has a face inclined at about 45 degrees to catch reflected light.

Beads and blades are by far the most common types of front sights, but many other forms have evolved, particularly for target shooting. I have seen beads suspended on wire in a globe, crosswires in a globe, circular front sights that are designed to encircle the bullseye for correct aim, etc.

A great fault of the metallic front sight is that it shoots away from the light. Worst offender is the unblackened gold bead. When the sun strikes it, it forms a false center which the shooter aims by. The same phenomenon is present to some degree with a red plastic or ivory sight. Even a blackened flat-top blade shows the same annoying deviation to a slight extent.

Most accurate form of front sight is the square-top blade in a dead black that reflects a minimum of light. When used with a good aperture sight on a black-and-white target it should be held at 6 o'clock. Then, shooting from a bench rest with a very accurate rifle, a good rifleman should group his shots into about 2 in. at 100 yd. The same rifle fittted with a 2½X hunting scope should group into about 1½ in. A 10X target-type scope should get him groups running around 1 in.

But if he should take the same rifle, put a glittering gold bead on its front end, and shoot with an aperture rear sight, he'll be doing well to group in 4 in., and if he substitutes the run-of-the-mine buckhorn open sight he'll get groups around 6 in. And all this difference is in a rifle with unvarying accuracy potential.

No rifle is better than its sights. The finest .270 or .30/06 that ever came out of the factory is at best a 200-yd. deer rifle if fitted with a big, glittering gold bead in front and an open sight in the rear — even in the hands of a crack shot with keen eyes. In the hands of a fair shot with poor eyes, it is about a 100-yd. rifle.

A fine .22 Hornet or .222 Remington fitted with an open rear sight is little better as a varmint rifle than a .22 rimfire because the human eye behind open sights is just about a 75-100-yd. eye on small, neutral-colored objects like woodchucks and prarie dogs. A .22 Hornet with a scope of good definition has a much greater sure-hitting range than a .220 Swift with iron sights.

No one can shoot any better than he can see, and the sight that enables the rifleman to aim quickly and exactly enables him to become a deadly shot.

CHAPTER XI

Games Teach Shotgun Skill

Traps and skeet shooting at a gun club
will give the beginner the best start
toward accuracy in the field

P ROBABLY the best and easiest method of acquiring shotgun skill
is to start with good instruction at a gun club where either traps
or skeet are shot, just as the best way to learn golf is to begin with an
instructor. Also beneficial is the shooting of clay targets thrown from
a hand trap, particularly if the young shooter has a good shot along
as a coach.

In these days of short seasons and limited bags, it is usually impossible for a tyro to get enough practice on game to develop any real
skill. In many sections, for instance, the pheasant is the only gamebird available to most gunners — and the pheasant season lasts only
five days, with the limit two cocks a day. The lad who shoots only
under such circumstances can expect to be a grandfather before he
becomes a good shot.

The young shooter is often understandably reluctant about beginning at a gun club, where he and his scores will be under the eyes of
strangers. He is fumbling and inept, and he is both impressed and
discouraged by the fancy-looking trap and skeet guns and by the
shooting jackets plastered with tabs announcing that their wearers
have broken 25 straight, 50 straight, 100 straight. What he doesn't
consider is that every veteran was once a beginner, too — a novice
just as clumsy as he. He doesn't realize that the old-timers welcome
new blood in the shooting game and make willing coaches.

Another advantage to the tyro in shooting at a gun club is that even if he gets no coaching he can learn much by just watching. No matter what sport a person is interested in — shooting, golf, tennis, swimming, or what have you — he can gain a great deal by observing how skillful performers operate.

Squad at traps. Here the target, unlike skeet, moves at an unpredictable angle.

The first time I ever shot a round of traps I simply picked up a gun, walked up to my station, and started shooting. I broke 16 clays (out of a possible 25), which isn't so hot. I shot again and broke 13. That would never do! Figuring I must be doing just about everything wrong, I watched good trapshooters for a while. The next time I took a whirl at traps I broke 22. The only instruction I'd had came from watching.

There are two principal clay-target games in this country — traps and skeet. Each is shot all over the United States, and most fairly large communities have skeet or trap clubs, or clubs that feature both games. As anybody can see by glancing at the accompanying sketches, the two games are quite different.

Traps is shot from five positions 3 yd. apart at single birds that come at varying angles out of a trap house at the call of the shooter. After

95

each string of five shots, the shooter moves to another station, and so on until he has shot from all five. Thus he gets varying angles, since a bird that presents a straightaway from one station is in sharply angled flight at another.

In ordinary singles shooting, the targets come out of the trap house 16 yd. from the gun, and the average trap shooter breaks them at about 33 yd. If he is a fast man with a gun, the good trap shot may break his birds as close in as 30 yd. If he is slow, he may hit them at 35 or 36. If he gets the jitters and freezes up — something that happens at times to all but the iron-nerved experts — he may break (more likely miss) some targets at 40 yd. or even farther, since they fly 50 yd. from the trap house and 66 yd. from the shooter.

The mechanics of 16-yd. singles are simple. The shooter takes his place at his station and mounts his gun with his cheek firm on the comb and his eyes right down the rib. He trains the muzzle on the spot where the bird is to appear, then calls "Pull!" The·bird, tripped by electricity, flashes out almost simultaneously with the call. The gunner swings up with the target and, without slowing his swing in the slightest, passes it and presses his trigger. If he has tracked in the right path, if he gets far enough ahead or above, if he doesn't slow or stop his swing, the target breaks as the shot charge strikes it. Flights vary from straightaways to fairly sharp right and left obliques. Shots are much like those the upland gunner gets when birds come up ahead of a dog, because the targets, like most upland gamebirds, are always rising.

Trapshooting is excellent practice for the upland gunner, but it isn't *perfect* practice. For one thing, the trap man has his gun mounted and his cheek on the comb before he calls for his bird. For another, he knows exactly when his target will appear and from what spot. True, he doesn't know the angle it will take, but if he is relaxed, doesn't try to outguess the trap, and busts them as they pop up, he'll find one angle no more difficult than another.

Traps will teach him swing and timing that will pay off in the field. One flaw of such shooting, from the standpoint of the bird hunter, is that the target isn't a pheasant or a quail. The clay starts off fast and then slows down, whereas the gamebird gets off slowly and picks up speed. The pheasant, for example, gets off the ground like an icewagon with wings, but picks up speed as he goes. At 50 yd. he is making knots. But at that distance the clay target is falling to the ground.

Another form of traps is single shooting at handicap distances. The individual shooters are put back according to their skill. One man may shoot at 16 yd., another at 25.

"Quail walk," where targets are released behind shooter, to keep him guessing.

Perhaps the most difficult of all clay-target games is doubles. Two birds come out of the trap house simultaneously 16 yd. from the gun, each on a fixed course, and it is up to the shooter to break both. He takes the straightaway first, then the angled bird. Knocking that second off before it hits the ground is no cinch. But it trains you for doubles in the field.

The man who simply wants to acquire some skill in handling his gun can shoot respectable scores at traps with practically any sort of scattergun that is bored modified or tighter. Most special trap guns are bored full choke (70 percent or more), because they are used at handicap rises as well as at the 16-yd. rise; but for 16-yd. targets alone, a modified barrel (55-60 percent) is all anyone needs.

The day before I wrote these lines, I shot a round with a Winchester Model 21 skeet gun with 26-in. barrels. I used the left (Skeet No. 2) barrel, approximately modified choke. I missed my first target because I tried to outguess the trap. I then broke the next 24 — and most of them were powdered. Actually, the fast shot who uses a full-choke barrel for 16-yd. targets alone is handicapping himself.

The special trap guns are usually long of barrel — 30 in. if pumps, and 30 or 32 in. if singles like the famous Ithaca single-barreled trap guns. They are generally bored full choke or improved-modified, and have raised or ventilated ribs and two sights. Only Ithaca now makes a single-barreled trap gun, but Winchester, Remington, and Ithaca make pumps stocked and equipped for trapshooting.

If the trapshooter has but one gun and plans to shoot doubles, this weapon, of course, must be either a repeater or a double. Automatics are not used at traps because the ejected shells bother the man at the shooter's right (shooting is in squads of five), and gimmicks like the Weaver-Choke, Cutts Comp, and POWer-PAC are not in order since their muzzle blast would give the others on the squad the screaming meemies. (Both variable-choke devices and auto loaders are legal in skeet.) The Winchester Model 21 double-barreled trap gun is popular, particularly for doubles shooting.

Since the targets are always rising, and since the gunner mounts his piece and gets his cheek down on the comb before he calls for a bird, the trap gun generally has a longer and straighter stock than a field gun. A gun so stocked shoots high — in effect, has a built-in lead for the rising targets. I find, though, that in traps I can take my regular Winchester Model 21 (which I use for skeet, pheasants, quail, etc.), place my cheek so I see more barrel than I would for skeet, and do as well with it as I can with anything. The casual trapshooter does not need a special gun, nor, in my opinion, is he greatly handicapped without one.

Skeet is a relative newcomer among clay-target games, having been invented in the 1920's by the late William Harnden Foster, who

98

became skeet editor of *Outdoor Life*. Many will disagree with me, but I think it highly probable that skeet is better practice for the field shot than is trapshooting. It's a faster and more spectacular game, and presents a much greater variety of shots and angles.

The skeet layout has two houses which contain traps for throwing birds. They're called the "high house," and the "low house," since one starts its targets high, the other low. The targets from each house always follow the same path, but the shooter gets different angles by moving around a semicircle and shooting at seven stations, starting at the high house and ending at the low house. There's another station, No. 8, in front of the semicircle and directly between the high house

Informal shooting at targets thrown from a hand trap is extremely valuable in training a shooter to follow the flight of a bird.

and the low house. He shoots a pair of singles at each station, one from the high house, one from the low. Angles vary from straightaways and slightly angling incomers at Stations 1 and 7, to shots that are approaching right angles or are true right angles at Stations 4 and 5. At the forward station, No. 8, the targets come almost directly toward the shooter — shots that are sometimes duplicated in the duck blind. The two shots at Station 8 are the bugaboo of the beginner, but actually are easy once the technique is learned.

The skeet gun is not mounted before the bird is called for. This, along with the sharper angles, greater variety of shots, and greater apparent speed, makes the game of skeet a natural for the man who wants to be sharp in the field. Unlike traps, skeet mixes singles and doubles in the same round. After the gunner has taken his Station 8 targets, he shoots pairs of doubles at Stations 1, 2, 6, and 7. He cannot tarry. Curiously, the beginner usually scores better at doubles than at singles because he knows he has to shoot fast; most skeet targets are missed because they are ridden out until they drop below the shot pattern.

Any good upland gun is satisfactory for skeet if the shooter is not out to become a tournament hotshot. I have done most of my skeet shooting with a couple of Winchester Model 21 skeet guns, one a 12 and one a 16, and I have also shot a good deal with an Ithaca 20

Skeet provides a wide variety of shots. Gunner here is at Station 4, with clay moving at about right angles to his line of aim.

gauge double, bored improved cylinder and modified. All three guns are stocked just alike — 1½ x 2¼ x 14¼ in. I must admit, however, that I have shot consistently higher scores with a Remington Model 11-'48 skeet gun with a ventilated rib. Why, I cannot say.

Probably the most efficient of all skeet guns is the automatic. The Remington Sportsman-'48 is becoming a favorite, as were the old Remington Model 11 and the Browning. An automatic is easier to use than a pump on double targets (although many fine shots use the Winchester, Ithaca, and Remington pumps) and the automatic softens recoil. Most top skeet-shots use either the Cutts Compensator with the spreader tube or the POWer-PAC with the short-range tube. Neither gives wider patterns than the special skeet borings of automatic and pump skeet guns, but many believe that the patterns are more regular. And these compensating devices have the virtue of further softening recoil.

There is skeet competition in a variety of gauges: all-bore (12 or 16 gauge); 20 gauge; small-bore (the .410 or 28 gauge with ¾ oz.

of shot); and subsmall-bore (the .410 with ½ oz.). Many skeet enthusiasts own a whole battery of guns so they can take part in all events.

The man who simply wants to be a good gun handler and has no yen to lug home cups and medals can do pretty well in all his shooting with one gun, and he may possibly be a better all-round field and duck shot if he sticks to one. My 12 gauge Winchester Model 21 has two sets of barrels — one set bored Skeet No. 1 and No. 2 (about improved cylinder and modified), the other set bored modified and improved-modified. By changing barrels I can make respectable scores at any kind of trap-shooting, at skeet, on upland game and waterfowl. A pump gun with a 26 or 28-in. barrel bored modified is also an all-round gun, and if it has two inter-changeable barrels, one bored improved cylinder, the other bored full or improved-modified, its owner is all set.

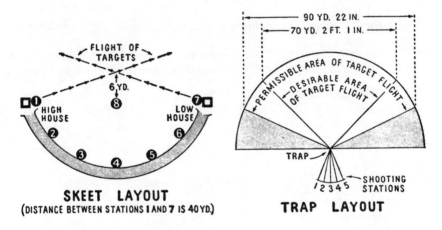

SKEET LAYOUT
(DISTANCE BETWEEN STATIONS 1 AND 7 IS 40 YD.)

TRAP LAYOUT

Like any gun nut, I am always looking for an excuse to get a new gun. In skeet I've recently used a Winchester Model 42 in .410; two Remington Model 11-'48's, one a 20, the other a 28; an Ithaca 20 gauge double; a Remington Model 870 skeet gun in 12 gauge; and a Winchester Model 21, also in 12 gauge. And I know perfectly well that my average would have been better if I'd stuck to one gun.

Besides the standard competitive games of trap and skeet, there are other less formal types of clay-target busting. Some clubs have towers that throw targets 50 ft. or more above the ground to provide practice in flight shooting. Another variation is the "quail walk" — the one at

Abercrombie & Fitch's shooting school on Long Island, N. Y., is a dilly. The shooter moves along a walk near which small traps have been placed. An attendant behind him trips 25 of about 35 possible targets. They come at the shooter, go away from him, fly in singles and pairs, move in the open and through trees. On a visit there, my son and I each broke 16, which, I was told, is about par for the skeet shooter on his first exposure. No one has ever broken a "straight" on the quail walk. The highest score is 23, and that was shot by a chap who practiced for months. It's a tough course, but it's the nearest thing to upland shooting I know.

Sadly enough, there is one great drawback to any clay-target shooting — the cost. A round of skeet or traps sets a man back anywhere from $2.50 to $3.50, including the price of a box of shells and 25 clay targets.

Breaking clays with a scattergun is by no means a 100 percent satisfactory substitute for the real thing. But it presents the one big chance for any man to become a genuinely good shotgun performer.

CHAPTER XII

Avoid Shooting Slumps

Every hunter comes upon days when he
can't seem to connect — Here are
diagnosis and treatment for this problem

IT IS depressing to relate, but there come times in the lives of most
shooting men when they couldn't hit a tethered goat on the back-
side with a violoncello. One day our pal Joe is poison; he knocks off,
neatly and thoroughly, everything that jumps. The next day, alas,
he can't hit anything. He is in a slump. Just why, he does not know.
He has been eating well and sleeping well. He is using the same gun
and the same ammunition. Still, he can't hit anything.

As his slump continues, he begins to slink through alleys. He avoids
his friends. He lies brooding and sleepless at night. Presently, for no
good reason known to man, his slump is over. Once again the sun is
bright, the sky is blue, and food tastes good. Joe hits what he shoots
at and he is happy.

Shooting slumps fascinate me because I have always been subject to
them. I take a morbid interest in mine and those of my friends. My
own slumps are far worse with a shotgun than with a rifle. Sometimes
I shoot a rifle better than at other times, but I never get very sour with
anything that has sights on it. In the days when I lived in jackrabbit
country and did a lot of rifle shooting on running jacks, I had streaks
of being very lucky. Instead of missing a bouncing bunny by a few
inches I'd hit him, and I might do this several times in a row. I used
to lay this to luck — rightly. If, on the other hand, I struck days when
I made a long run of close misses on those small, fast targets, I was

philosophical about it. I knew that presently good luck would catch up with me. And it would.

With a scattergun, it is another story, and I can tell you some tales of shooting slumps that would make your flesh creep. The baffling thing about a slump with a shotgun is that it is exceedingly hard to put a finger on the cause. The rifleman worth his salt always calls his shots. His trained eye and mind have registered a picture of where his front bead of the reticle of his scope rested when the rifle went off. All target shooting and a high percentage of game shooting is at stationary marks. The sights are either properly aligned or they aren't — and that's that.

Even when shooting at a running animal, the good rifleman has the habit of calling his shot and he retains in his mind the image of his sight picture. If he leads by a foot when he lets off the first shot and shoots behind, he knows he has to lead by more the next time.

The shotgun man, though, has his eyes focused on the target and he pays far less attention to the muzzle of his gun — which is his front sight — than he does to the bird or to the clay target he is trying to hit. Hence errors can creep up on him unawares. He then flounders in the dark.

He may be changing his timing, slowing or stopping his swing, flinching, or failing to get his cheek down on the comb. Any of these things can turn a good shotgun shooter into a lousy one — and every one of them is hard to detect.

One of the easiest of all ways to bring on a string of misses is for the shotgunner to change his natural timing. Watch a squad shooting traps or skeet sometime and you will notice that each man shoots in his own particular "time." One may be faster than another and the spectator soon becomes conscious of each gunner's natural time. If a man shoots in that natural time he'll almost always hit. If he slows down or tries to speed up he'll almost always miss. An astute spectator quickly becomes conscious of this natural rhythm — probably more conscious of it than the fellow who is doing the actual shooting.

I know a young skeet shot who gets careless now and then and misses a target. When he does, he almost always misses the next one too, because he becomes angry and tries to break the second clay halfway to Station 8. Instead of shooting carefully and in his proper time, he shoots too quickly, out of time, and draws a zero on the score sheet.

I have seen fine trap shots try to change their timing, and the results were disastrous. One of them, when he is having an attack of jitters, can get so out of time that he will not shoot at some targets until they are 50 yd. out. Another, who had never broken a straight at skeet, found himself, after having broken 24 targets, taking his optional at Station 7. He called for the low-house bird, which comes up at waist level and sails straight away, looking as big as a bald eagle. My pal froze up so badly that he didn't shoot at the target until it was far beyond Station 8 and halfway to the net. Of course, he missed it.

One Sunday I was shooting a bit of skeet and one of the lads out was a college boy who is a crack shotgun pointer, a local hot shot. He brought his gal out to see him perform for the first time. Naturally he was trying to impress her. He broke his single targets so fast my tired old eyes could hardly pick them up before they were smoke. He shot at his doubles with such speed that it was hard to distinguish the two reports. But alas and alack, this fine young shot came up with the sad score of 19. Why? He was trying to speed up his shooting out of his natural time. It just can't be done successfully.

Why does timing go to pot? I believe the reasons are almost always psychological. Our trapshooter was too anxious to break them all and our skeet shot was too anxious to break his first straight. Both were suffering from a form of buck fever, but instead of being unable to press the trigger, our skeet lad was shooting too fast.

I remember once when my own timing went sour on game. I had just bought a Winchester Model 21 skeet gun. I knew that it threw a wider pattern than I'd ever used on Gambel's quail, and I was haunted by the fear that I was going to have to shoot very fast — before the birds got out of range. I managed to do some very fancy quail shooting but I couldn't hit a thing. Before long I was half convinced that the shells I was using didn't have any shot in them.

The pay-off came when I stood in my tracks and missed two easy straight-away shots at singles. Without moving I put a shell in my open-bored right barrel and aimed at the flat leaf of a pricklypear cactus near where the birds had been. It was 27 paces from where I stood and the shot riddled it.

I couldn't blame the gun. It was giving me plenty of pattern density. The sad and unpleasant truth was that I simply hadn't been getting that pattern *on* the quail. In trying to speed up my timing I had failed to get my cheek down on the comb and I shot over every bird I fired at. Convinced, then, that the birds couldn't fly through the patterns at the moderate ranges at which I was shooting, I began to take more time. And once I fell back into my natural rhythm the birds began to fall.

On another occasion I was hunting over a pointing dog with an elderly chap of whom I was very fond. I tried to let him get two chances at each cock pheasant before I shot. He missed a lot of birds, but, alas, so did I. Changing my timing made my shooting sour — this time, I believe, because I was slowing or stopping my swing. Whenever I went off by myself I averaged almost 100 percent on the pheasants, but when I tried to wait them out so my companion could shoot first I doubt that I averaged 30 percent. The moral seems to be that when you shoot out of your natural timing you are likely to miss. The reason may be nervousness, cautiousness, or trying to be good to a fellow shooter. Whatever the cause, though, the result is the same.

I get an enormous kick out of pheasant hunting. I was never fortunate enough to hunt ringnecks until 1948, when I immediately fell in love with the big, smart, gaudy birds. They are not difficult to hit. Every year I start out like a house afire. Then along in the middle of the season I go sour for anywhere from two days to a week.

Last season I was going great guns. I had never shot better in my life. Then it happened. I had been centering my birds, and when they came down they hit the ground as dead as Caesar. But when my slump came I either missed clean or caught my birds on the edge of the pattern so that they lit running. For three days I'd get about one pheasant in three shots — and even that showing was due largely to a good dog that ran the birds down.

Strangely enough, my shooting partner was also in a slump. The easier the shots, the surer we were to miss them. One sunny afternoon we both missed three fat cocks in succession. All were right under my dog's nose. All were straightaway shots and in the open.

What's the answer to that one?

Well, I think we were tired. Our reactions were slow and we were not swinging up fast enough to take those jumping pheasants. We were missing by shooting under. Those we did hit were farther out and had leveled off so that we were trying to drive shot into the vitals from the hind end and not getting pellets into the head and neck, as one does when the bird is still rapidly rising.

My cure was simple, but whether it had a physical or a psychological basis I cannot say. My field gun is a Winchester Model 21 in 12 gauge. It is bored modified and improved modified, has a pistol-grip buttstock, and weighs 7½ lb. In the family we have another Model 21, a 16 gauge that weighs a bit less than 7 lb. and has a straight grip. It is a high-shooting son-of-a-gun and poison on a jumping pheasant, which is a rapidly rising target. On skeet I have to fight it every shot if I'm to break 20, because I have to remember all the time to hold under the targets. When the pheasant slump continued I switched to it, and the next day I bounced three roosters with three shots.

How come? Was I swinging faster with the lighter gun — or getting the shot up and into the bird with the higher shot pattern? Or was the business purely psychological because I had cured my past slumps with the same gun? I do not know the answer.

I have cured some slumps, when I found I was shooting behind, by shifting to a lighter gun. I have also brought on slumps by changing to a heavier gun with a longer barrel. The heavier the gun and the longer the barrel, the slower the swing with the same amount of muscular effort. The man who has been using a 26-in. barrel and shifts to a 28 or 30-in. barrel will shoot behind unless he consciously takes extra pains to get farther ahead. Then, when he becomes lead-conscious, he tends to stop his swing. This shooting with a heavier gun is exactly the same thing as a high jumper trying to go over the crossbar while wearing lumberjack boots instead of light track shoes. He simply cannot jump as high with the heavy footgear as he can with the light.

I know a dozen people who hunt upland game with light, short-barreled guns for several weeks and then shift to heavy guns with long barrels for ducks. Without exception they do some rather sad shooting until their muscles make all the necessary adjustments.

It works the other way too. One of the finest shots I know, a chap who has broken 200 straight at both traps and skeet, hunted birds with me one year. He had been using heavy 12 gauge guns for his clay-target hunting. For birds he bought a 5½-lb. 20 gauge. He shot ahead of every crossing or angling bird and was in despair until he borrowed the sort of gun he was used to. From then on he was deadly.

One time I went into a dilly of a slump because of a sore shoulder. I was hunting pheasants with my light, short-barreled 12 gauge double. I wore only a cotton shirt and a shooting vest. Since a pheasant takes plenty of killing I was using maximum loads of 3¾ drams of powder and 1¼ oz. of No. 6 shot. In case anyone asks you, that combination kicks — and my gun has only a checkered wood butt, no recoil pad. All of a sudden I got up to my neck in quail. On my first shot I was out of position, and I fired before I got the gun to my shoulder. I was badly kicked and it hurt. The next shot hurt worse. By the time I had fired a third shot my whole arm was aching to the fingertips and I had a lump on my shoulder the size of a baseball. That first whack had ruptured a muscle, the doctor later told me, and I had what athletes call a Charley horse.

Every time my dog would come to a point I'd moan, "This is going to hurt." But I'd walk in and flush the bird. As I swung along, I'd dread the recoil and the pain that was to come, and of course when I shot I'd flinch — and miss. I couldn't hit a thing until I sewed a pad into my shirt and shifted to a 20 gauge with a soft-rubber recoil pad. As soon as I stopped aching I began to hit.

So if shooting out of natural time is a fine way to miss, developing a flinch is another guarantee of coming home with an empty game-bag. And so is feeling hurried and rushed and failing to get the cheek down on the comb, thus seeing too much barrel and overshooting.

When two people with a competitive urge hunt together, and each tries to beat the other to a bird, a lot of missing will result. Let them separate, and they'll usually begin to connect.

I ran into an amusing example of trying to beat the other guy to the shot and missing, and it involved not birds but deer. Two friends and I were horseback hunting up a long, grassy ridge in the Canelo Hills of southern Arizona years ago. The canyon on our left was bare except for a few scattered scrub oaks. Anyone with sense would *know* there were no deer there. Then a white-tailed buck pumped out from behind a tree about 150 yds. away.

We all piled off our horses, grabbed our rifles out of the scabbards, and blazed away — each afraid another guy would beat him to the buck. We were all in practice from shooting running jacks and the shot was easy. If any of us had been alone that deer would probably have dropped at the first shot. As it was we collectively rattled off nine shots and never touched him.

Many a time I have seen the same thing happen on gamebirds. The flustered man, the overanxious man, misses.

But the meanest and most insidious way of missing with the scattergun is slowing or stopping the swing. It is poisonously frustrating because it is so hard to detect. That's one reason why missing leads to more missing. You miss one bird. You then decide you'll center the next one that gets out. You are determined you'll have just the right lead. You slow your swing to be darned sure of it — and the bird sails on.

Not long ago I happened to look at a picture of a skeet layout and it dawned on me that the No. 3 low-house bird was a right-angle shot. "Tut, tut," I thought, "I haven't been leading that bird enough. I have been shooting when the muzzle is 1 ft. ahead of it. By all logic I should lead it 3 ft." Why I thought so I'll never know because I hadn't missed that shot in years.

So, taking particular pains to lead the bird 3 ft., I went out and shot *behind* it three times in succession. Why? Determined to lead exactly 3 ft., I'd been stopping my swing. Then I said to heck with it, swung fast, shot when I was a little ahead and broke it.

I am assuming here, of course, that the lad who goes into a slump is a good shot, a man who places his feet right and has trained himself to get his head down and to put his stock to his face. Even this chap is not proof against slumps. Let him hunt on steep hillsides, and much of the time he cannot place his feet correctly. His swing will be cramped and he'll miss. Or he may put more clothes on, so that the fit of his gun is no longer right — his cheek being farther back on the comb — and he'll undershoot.

What to do when a slump strikes you? Instead of getting panicky about it, try to figure it out. If you're tired and your reactions are sluggish, take it easy and rest up. If you find yourself shooting behind, try shifting to a lighter gun with a shorter barrel. If you are feeling rushed and probably failing to get your head down, try counting 1-2-3 before you shoot.

Above all, don't monkey with your gunstock. If it has fitted you in the past, it fits you now. If you change the pitch or drop, you'll just have to get used to it all over again. I have a pal who has all the requisites of a crack trap shot except temperament. Let him shoot a bum score and he begins to monkey with the adjustable buttplate on his trap gun. The more he changes the drop, the more he misses.

Best thing I know of about slumps is that they do not last. If you don't worry about them, they'll usually go as mysteriously as they came. If you have sort of a good-luck piece it always helps — and it's my hunch that the effect of that straight-stocked 16 gauge of mine may be largely psychological. I have a friend who banishes slumps by wearing a ragged old red shirt. When his shooting falls off he puts it on. Then he hits because he *knows* he'll hit — and that is the most important thing of all.

JACK O'CONNOR'S
HANDBOOK FOR HUNTERS

BOOK 2

CHAPTER XIII

Long-Range Game Shooting

**Judgment is required to know when
to take a chance on a distant shot and
when to stalk closer**

BY JACK O'CONNOR

A GOOD deal of moonshine has been written about shooting big game
at long range. On one hand we have the boys of limited experience — most of it acquired in brush and forest — who say that anyone who claims to have knocked off a deer at over 150 yd. is a liar.
They haven't done it, and they haven't seen it done, so they won't
believe anyone does it. At the other extreme are the imaginative
citizens who never kill a head of game at less than 300 yd. and find
a 500-yd. shot just routine.

I remember a story written by one of these long-range experts about
a hunt in northern British Columbia. He and his guide saw a grizzly
at about 500 yd. Did they pause to find out what the bear was doing,
which way he was headed, how they could get closer? They did not.
Instead our hero sat down, fed a cartridge into the chamber of his
trusty .375 Magnum, and started tossing bullets in the direction of
the bear. They finally got the grizzly — or so the story went — but
only after wounding it and following it into brush, a chore I have
done but do not relish.

Another type of big-game shot would have stalked that grizzly to
within 25 yd., and would not have shot until he saw the whites of its
eyes.

For my part, I prefer a sensible median between trying to shoot an animal across a township and getting close enough to ram the rifle muzzle down its throat. Most astute procedure is to do execution at from 75 to 150 yd., if circumstances permit. Usually it isn't difficult to stalk to such a distance, but the closer one gets to the game the more chance there is of disturbing it. At 100-150 yd., a rifleman worthy of the name should be able to place his bullet within from 2 to 3 in. of where he holds, and he can kill as well as if he were within 50 ft. At that distance, the hunter is not nearly so liable to get grizzly fever as he would if close enough to hit the bear with a rock.

If I were a guide and had a dude out who even *looked* as if he wanted to shoot a grizzly at 500 yd., I'd wrap his rifle around his neck. Anyone who hunts dangerous game — be it grizzlies or Alaska

Custom built .300 long-range rifle on a Winchester Model 70 action. Its "Blown out" cartridge takes 80 gr. of No. 4350 powder and a 180-gr. bullet. Dunlap muzzle brake reduces recoil to about that of a .257.

brown bears in North America, or buffaloes, lions, or leopards on the African plains — has no business taking long-range shots. Promiscuous long-range shooting by gents without judgment results in too many wounded animals getting away, and in the case of dangerous game, too much chance somebody will have his leg chewed off.

Legitimate shooting at long range requires, first of all, the rather poorly distributed commodity called judgment, something which many of us, alas, do not have. Before a rifleman takes a pop at an animal beyond his sure hitting range, he should pause and ask himself what will happen if he wounds the beast. Once I was riding back toward camp with a trigger-happy character when he saw a big bull moose, with enormous snowy-white antlers, standing on the far side of a muskeg meadow. He was about 400 yd. away and right at the edge of heavy timber. This citizen jumped off his horse and before you could say glockenspiel he had fired offhand. I heard the plunk of the bullet on a water-filled stomach, and the bull faded into the timber. We found no blood, but we did find some hairs cut off by the bullet. We tracked the bull about a quarter of a mile but it grew dark back in the timber and we had to return to our horses and ride to camp. As far as I could see, our boy suffered no remorse. But all he'd done was donate some meat to the wolves.

That was no time for a long-range shot. Here's why: 1. The hunter couldn't get into a steady position. 2. A moose is a big, tough animal that is very difficult to kill at 400 yd. with a .30/06 — or with any weapon short of a 37 mm. cannon. 3. The bull was standing at the edge of the timber and would be out of sight in one jump. 4. Only a few minutes of light remained.

But if our hunter had caught the bull in an open basin above timberline where it couldn't get out of sight until he had a chance for a dozen shots, *and* if he were then able to get into a steady position, *and* if he were desperate for a moose trophy, he might have been justified in taking a chance on a long shot.

Just what is a long-range shot on big game? Defined conservatively, it is any shot made beyond the ordinary point-blank range of the rifle in use. And that means any shot in which the bullet will fall more than 4 in. below the line of sight and where allowance for drop is necessary.

Take an iron-sighted rifle of the .30/30 class sighted in to put the bullet at point of aim at 150 yd. (which is the usual practice). With such a rifle, any range beyond about 190 yd. (at which point the bullet has dropped 4 in.) can be considered long range. With a scope-sighted .30/06 using the 180-gr. bullet and sighted in to hit point of aim at 200 yd., anything over 250 yd. is long range. With a .30/06 scope-sighted for 250 yd. with the 150-gr. bullet, anything beyond about 290 yd. is long range — and the same figures apply to the .300 Magnum with the 180-gr. bullet.

With a .270, scope-sighted for 275 yd., anything beyond 325 is long range. Big-game rifles of still higher velocity — like the Weatherby series of .270, 7 mm. and .300 Magnum — have a still longer point-blank range. In their case the critical point — the 4-in. bullet drop — is about at 350 yd. — or 25 farther than with the standard .270.

114

And let's remember that even with the flat-shooting .300 Weatherby Magnum at 350 yd., a shot is a good one if it lands in the chest cavity; after all, the human being behind the rifle is still a human being, with human tremors and shakes and wobbles.

Great aids to long-range shooting are a flat-shooting, accurate rifle and a scope of good definition (so the rifleman can see exactly where he is holding). Then the combination should be sighted in for the longest possible point-blank range, so that the rise of the bullet above the line of sight will not cause midrange misses. That means, if the target is a big-game animal, that the bullet should not rise more than 4 in. — possibly 5 — above the line of sight. The less guessing about holdover a man has to do, the better off he is. Even the most experienced and skillful riflemen lay plenty of eggs. That is why — if there is any possibility at all of a shot at longer than usual range — a hunter is a sucker to sight in a .30/30 for 100 yd. or a .270 or .30/06 for 200.

It's much wiser, if a long-range shot is likely to present itself, to sight in for the longest possible range and to use a scope of good definition. A 4X is a fine compromise for this "if" sort of hunting. For open-country shooting exclusively — when a shot at under 150 yd. is the exception — a lot of very shrewd riflemen are going to the 6X scopes.

The importance of sighting in for the longest possible range was impressed on me many years ago, when I did a lot of hunting for the smart and elusive little Arizona white-tail deer in southern Arizona and northern Sonora, Mexico. Most of my shots were from hillside to hillside or across canyons at longish and undetermined range. I found I could hit the white-tails better with a .270 than with a .30/06 because of the former's somewhat higher velocity and flatter trajectory; better with a .270 sighted in for 275 or 300 yd. than with one sighted in for 200; and better with a 4X scope than with a 2½X. The reason? When a buck bounces out across the canyon, my instinct (and I beileve everyone's instinct) is to blast away directly at him instead of figuring the angles and holding over.

I remember very well the buck that made me a convert. He got up at undetermined range across a rough, rocky, and very steep canyon and started picking them up and putting them down. Because the terrain was rough he couldn't go very fast, and my lead was perfect.

115

I could see dust fly all around him. Finally he went down on about the ninth shot.

I found several bullet burns on the bottom of his chest and belly. My .270 was sighted in for 200 yd., and the buck was probably over 300 yd. away — beyond the point-blank range as I had sighted in. I couldn't possibly have killed the buck with a dead-on hold, and I wouldn't have killed him at all if I hadn't jerked the trigger and made the fatal bullet fly high.

Bert Rigall, Alberta guide, uses a rope loop to steady his knees when he tries a long shot from the sitting position.

It is usually possible to get close to many animals, particularly in open mountains where they can be located and stalked by a concealed approach from behind a ridge. But some have to be taken at long range. Those little Arizona white-tails are an example. Mule deer in many sections are found in open country, where frequently they cannot be approached, and antelope are almost always open-country game. In many cases it is the better part of wisdom for the hunter to take a long shot at a standing animal than to attempt to get closer, and have to take the risk of a running shot.

In broken-up country, antelope — like wild sheep — can be closely approached. But if the country is flat and open, or even gently rolling — with the top of one little rise half a mile or more from another —

116

antelope are a long-range proposition. In some areas the hunter will see ten elk at 300-400 yd. for every one he sees at lesser range. If he is going to fill the home freezer he is going to have to do some long-range shooting. Much of Idaho's Selway country is like that — great brushy ridges cut by enormous canyons.

Judgment of range is by no means easy. Animals look closer in good light than in poor, farther away when seen from above or below than when seen on the level. They look closer across a canyon with no intervening objects, closer across a perfectly flat, level plain with no vegetation.

I can remember some astonishingly bad guesses I have made. Once in the Yukon I came to a river bed. Across a perfectly flat bar, glistening white in bright sunlight, I saw a wolf. I estimated the range to be about 300 yd. and held accordingly. The bullet struck in the sand at least 100 yd. short. Part of my error stemmed from the bright light and the flat sand, but most of it was due, I believe, to the fact that I was used to shooting at the much smaller coyote.

Another time I fired several shots at a black bear high above me on a northern British Columbia mountainside and never even came close enough to scare it much. The members of my party went into a huddle to dope out the reason for the misses. They concluded that the bear had been much farther away than I thought — 700 or 800 yd. I decided I'd been crossed up by the fact that the bear was a cub, and that instead of underestimating the range, as my pals thought, I had grossly overestimated it.

Now and then a hunter runs into a guide who is an expert rifle shot and a good judge of range. Such a guide is well worth listening to. But many guides, while they've killed a lot of big game, have done it only at short range. Often they are not expert riflemen or particularly good judges of range. Because of these factors, they chronically overestimate range, and to many anything over 150 yd. is 400 yd. I once killed a ram that my guide swore was "over a quarter of a mile away." I held dead on with the .270 and hit about where I held. The ram was probably about 250-275 yd. from the muzzle. An antelope that a guide swore was 500 or 600 yd. away was likewise killed with a dead-on hold, and the range was no more than 300 yd.

There are two methods of arriving at a fair estimate of range. One, if the terrain permits, is to divide the intervening country with your eye into 100-yd. units. Of course, that calls for out-of-season practice over measured terrain. Golf players, with their trained eyes, are usually very good at guessing hunting ranges. The other is to use some sort of a range-finding scope reticle in comparison with the depth of the animal's chest.

In taking a long shot, this youth uses the ridge comb as a rest and his rolled-up jacket as a pad. Such a set-up provides nearly all the advantages of a bench rest.

Sad to say, both methods are only approximate, but they do save the rifleman from extremely bad errors. If game animals came in standard sizes, the range-finder reticle would be quite efficient, but alas, they do not. Deer measure from 14 to 20 in. from top of shoulder to bottom of brisket; adult antelope 16 or 17; a big ram or a goat from 20 to 22; an elk from 24 to 28; a bull moose from 30 to 40, with 36 being about the average of those I have measured; a coyote 8 or 9.

A range-finder reticle consiting of two horizontal crosswires is available in Weaver scopes. The space between the wires subtends 6 minutes of angle. If the chest area of a full-grown deer fills that space, you can estimate that he is around 300 yd. away. I have also used a 4-minute Lee dot in a 2½X scope and found it useful.

Last long-range shot I made was on an antelope. He was standing on a slope across a wide, shallow basin in northeast Wyoming and looking at me. I thought he was about 400 yd. away, but when I divided the intervening ground into 100-yd. units it added up to about 500 yd. The bullet I was using would drop about 3 ft. at that

Weaver's Range-Finder scope sight has two horizontal crosshairs. Relationship of animal's body to the space betwen the hairs indicates approximate range.

distance. I got a good steady rest and held the crosswires above his shoulder for a distance 1½ times the depth of his body. I squeezed the trigger and the buck went down. My companions and I paced off the range and it came out about 485 yd.

The longest shot I ever saw made on a big-game animal was in the far north and the victim was a big bull caribou. A companion and I had been hunting a week with no luck. We'd been out of camp meat for days, so it was a foregone conclusion that if we ran into any legal and edible game, it would have a tough time.

Then with binoculars we picked up a bull caribou about two miles away. He was toward the bottom of an absolutely open, gently sloping basin, and since caribou have poor eyes it looked as if stalking him would be easy. But this bull was an exception. When we were still much too far away, he spied us and started to move off.

"He's spooked," the guide said. "Better shoot."

119

While I was protesting that this was no good because the bull was too far off, my pal opened up with his scope-sighted .270. The first shot, fired with the horizontal crosswire held even with the bull's back, hit well below his feet. The second shot, held the same way to confirm the first, also landed there. The fourth shot hit the caribou. My pal had aimed at a rock that seemed to be 7 or 8 ft. over the bull's back. The caribou moved slowly off, getting farther and farther away. Apparently the eighteenth shot was also a hit. The bull moved perhaps 100 yd. farther and lay down in some willows with only his antlers showing.

Since my friend and the guide would lose sight of the bull in going over to finish him, I stayed on the hillside to signal if the animal moved. After a long, long time the two got up to the caribou and finished it with a shot in the neck.

Then I decided to see how far away that bull was. About half the distance in a straight line to the bull was downhill, the other half uphill. By the time I got to the carcass I had used up 1,823 paces. The bull was at least 700 yd. away when first hit and surely not less than 1,200 yd. distant when another shot connected.

We had our meat, but I still doubt that the shots should have been taken at all. The caribou was simply too far away.

On the other hand, my pal had a very accurate .270 with a 6X scope, and he was an expert shot. We needed the meat, and the animal was in an open basin where we could shoot at him quite a few times while he was trying to escape.

Such wild-eyed shots are rare exceptions, though. The usual long-range shot is at from 300 to 450 yd. at a standing and undisturbed animal.

Actually it is easier to make a neat, clean kill from a good rest on a stationary target at long range than it is to make one from the offhand position at 200 yd.

For real long-range shooting, the hunter should get into the steadiest position possible. Now and then the terrain permits him to shoot prone with a tight sling, but that's quite rare in big-game hunting. The long-range big-game shot faces exactly the same problem as the varmint hunter who likes to knock off chucks at from 300 to 400 yd., and he should follow his example of using a rifle rest at every opportunity. Few people can hold steady enough, even from a good solid sitting position, to be certain of placing a bullet in the chest cavity of deer or antelope out at 400 yd. or more.

In the Canadian north I usually wear a down jacket, and many times I have rolled it up and used it on a stone or hummock for a steady rest. In Wyoming antelope hunting, I have used the same rolled-up jacket on clumps of sage. Once in a while a man can put a "10 gallon" hat in the crotch of a tree and use it as a rest. The rifleman should never lay the fore-end of the rifle on anything hard, because if he does the rifle will jump up from the hard surface and his shot will be high.

My longest shot at a mountain sheep was made at a nice Dall ram in the White River country of the Yukon. My guide and I were behind a ridge almost sharp enough to shave with. I found a ledge on which I could sit, and a notch in the sharp ridge that I could stick the rifle through and rest it on my down jacket. There was even a little ledge on which I could rest my right elbow. All in all, it was a crude, natural, but very effective bench rest. I could hold like a rock, and my only problem was that of judging range and dropping a bullet into a vital area of the ram. I hit him the first shot.

Just as the finest practice for the running-game shooter is popping at galloping jackrabbits, the best possible practice for the long-range big-game shot is long-range shooting of woodchucks, predatory hawks, crows, and coyotes.

This essay is not an endorsement of promiscuous long-range shooting. From a humanitarian standpoint, the less of it done — even by a good shot — the better. But the time does come when circumstances are right, and then an expert rifleman can save his bacon by making a hit at long range.

First of all, the animal should be non-dangerous. He should be in the open so bullet effect can be judged and the first shot followed up with others if it is not fatal. The hunter should have an accurate, flat-shooting rifle, sighted in for the longest possible range which will not cause midrange misses. He should be able to judge range fairly well by mentally marking off the distances in 100-yd. units or by comparing the size of an animal with a reticle of known value. He should know the drop at various ranges of the bullet he is using, and if his memory is poor he should affix the data to the buttstock of his rifle with transparent waterproof tape. He should shoot from the steadiest position he can assume, and then he should squeeze the trigger and hope for the best.

Never should he attempt a shot from an unsteady position, nor when the animal can get out of sight quickly. He should avoid shooting at long range if it seems possible to move within his sure hitting range, even if he has to come back the next day to make the stalk. When he does try long-range shooting he should use every means at his command to do the job exactly right!

CHAPTER XIV

Sit and You'll Hit

The sitting position is the best
compromise between prone and offhand
for most shooting

BY JACK O'CONNOR

O N the plains and in the mountains, the sitting position is the
most useful of them all when you're after big game. It isn't
quite as steady as the prone, so your shooting will be a little less accurate. It isn't quite as fast as the offhand when you have an easy-to-
hit target, but it's a lot faster for a *precise* shot at a difficult mark. It
doesn't put the line of sight quite as high above the ground as the
kneeling position, but it's a heck of a lot steadier. Finally, it can be
used under a greater variety of conditions than any other reasonably
steady position.

I do about three-fourths of my practicing from the sitting position,
the rest offhand. I use the kneeling position very rarely, and my prone
position is usually not the conventional type — I rest the rifle's forearm on a rolled-up jacket placed on a stone, a log, or something of
the sort.

In the mountain and canyon country of the Southwest, where I
grew up, the usual shots at deer are across canyons that may be from
150 to 400 yd. wide. When game pops into view, the thing to do is
to sit down instantly, get on, and touch her off. But *sit!* Once I sat
down and got off a shot so quickly at a running buck that my companion, who was looking the other way and didn't see the deer,

thought the gun had gone off accidentally. From my first sight of the deer until it lay dead three seconds may have elapsed.

On the other hand, I remember taking an offhand shot at a buck drowsing under a tree like a sleepy horse. I was in waist-high chaparral and, of course, could not have seen him if I sat down. The buck

The sitting position with sling minimizes wobble. So does proper placement of the left arm as explained in the text.

was between 250 and 300 yd. away. I assumed my best target stance but my sights wavered all over the buck and 20 or 30 ft. of the surrounding territory. It must have taken me a good minute to get off the shot. If I had been able to sit down I could have knocked off that buck within seconds.

When I used to shoot a lot of running antelope and black-tail jackrabbits, I'd sit down if the target was much more than 100 yd. away. Sitting is not as flexible as the offhand or even the kneeling position, but it is flexible enough to cope with most running game in open country. Its major hazard is that you may sit on something that wasn't meant to be sat on, but that seems of small consequence when a buck mule deer with 10 points and a 38-in. spread is on the opposite side of the canyon.

I have carried home many a bruise from sharp rocks or sticks, but

124

my worst punishment came, not when I was after a lordly buck, but when I ran into a whole flock of jackrabbits. I came over a ridge and there, on the opposite side, were five or six big juicy antelope jacks. Automatically I went into a sit — on a pile of cholla balls. Imagine about 10,000 No. 10 fishhooks sticking out of an egg and you have it. I had 7,692 cactus thorns in my rear end and I slept on my stomach for a week.

The sitting position is not only fast and fairly steady but, best of all, it can be used — unlike prone or kneeling — to shoot across or down a hillside. For mountain hunting it is the business. In plains hunting it is very useful for a steady shot when no rest is available and you can't lie prone because grass and weeds are too high or because cactus, thorns, or sharp rocks make lying down hazardous.

Just how accurately can a lightweight, scope-sighted hunting rifle be shot from the sit? A good rifleman should be able to keep three-fourths of his shots inside a 10-in. bull at 300 yd. Now and then he'll score a possible, but ordinarily from one to three or four shots will wander out of the black. They should not, however, from that position, be *far* out.

Holding an 8 or 9½-lb. hunting rifle steady is harder than holding down a 10½ or 11½-lb. target rifle. At 200 yd., if our boy is holding and squeezing well, practically *all* the shots should be pretty well centered in the 10-in. black. On occasion I've shot such groups running around 4 in. And once, with a scope-sighted .270, I grouped 5 shots at 200 yd. that measured only about 2¾ in. across. But I don't kid myself that in these cases it wasn't about 85 percent luck.

Be that as it may, a good shot with a 4X scope on an accurate rifle will kill more jackrabbits and woodchucks at 200 yd. from the sit than he'll miss. And even at 300 yd., with a scope of 8X or 10X, he'll make a surprising proportion of one-shot kills. Since errors of aim from the sitting position tend to be horizontal rather than vertical, there is more leeway on a big-game animal than on a varmint, so it's no astounding feat to place all shots in the forward half on an elk or caribou at 400 yd.

In shooting game — be it jackrabbit, woodchuck, white-tail deer, grizzly bear, or what have you — there are no close 4's. Only the 3's count. It is better by far to get in one well-aimed, well-held, well-placed shot from the sit than to get in three or four poorly aimed, poorly held, poorly placed shots or misses offhand. No time to sit? I have seen many a man miss three or four shots at standing game that he could have killed dead if he'd taken a second to plant his posterior on the earth.

Recently I read about an African lion hunter who, when faced with

1. In this series of pictures O'Connor shows how to get into a Whelen-type sling to make the sitting position even steadier. First he slips left arm through loop preformed in sling to suit his build (left). Then with loop pushed high on his arm, he brings left hand over the strap (right) and places it up against the fore-end swivel, tightening the sling.

a charge, always sat down if the grass was not too high. He figured on getting off one well-held, well-aimed shot and knocking the lion for a loop.

I remember one sad occasion when I elected to shoot a deer from offhand rather than take a second longer and drop into the sit. I came around a point and saw, about 200 yd. away, a beautiful buck that had apparently heard me and got out of his bed. He was poised there — alert, beautiful, his gray body outlined sharply against a dark timber background, the sun glittering on the polished points of his antlers. (The ones that get away usually look big, but I'll swear that buck had 18 points.) He saw me as I saw him, and I was afraid he'd

126

scram into the timber before I could drop down into the sit, so I slowly lifted my rifle — and shot right over the top of his back. On the target range I'd have got a close 4 for that one, but he got away just as cleanly as if I'd shut my eyes and missed him by 50 ft.

When the uninstructed beginner first tries the sitting position, he almost always makes one principal mistake. He sits up too straight and puts his wobbly elbows right on his wobbly kneecaps. That position is little steadier, if any, than offhand. The secret of a good sitting position is to lean forward and put the flat of the left arm, just above the elbow, against the flat of the shin just below the left knee. Feet should be well apart and feet and ankles relaxed. I have often read that "the heels should be dug into the ground." That's the poorest advice I know of, since the digging induces a tremor. The only time the rifleman should jam his heels into the ground is when he's shooting from a steep hillside and has to dig in to keep from skidding.

Everyone, I believe, has to work out the minor details of his own sitting position for himself. A man with a paunch, for instance, cannot bend forward as far as a flat-bellied youth. Some riflemen prefer crossed legs rather than outstretched ones. For me, though, the key to a good solid sitting position is the relationship of left arm and shin, as described above. What happens to the right arm is relatively unimportant, just so the position feels comfortable and *relaxed.* The natural tension of the back muscles will pull the upper arms against the shin and bring equilibrium and relative steadiness.

In no position should a rifleman try to hold by main strength. He should always feel relaxed. The harder a man tries to hold, the more tense he becomes; and the more tension, the greater the wobble.

My own besetting sin is tenseness. I often catch myself bearing down, determined to hold that damned rifle steady if I have to squeeze it in two at the grip — and when I hold like that, the old musket wobbles all over the target. Then I must *deliberately* loosen up.

I am convinced that the difference between the ordinary good rifleman and the superlative one is not that the latter has better eyes or muscles, or is smarter or better-looking, but simply that he can relax, even when picking off the biggest buck he ever saw at 350 yd. or firing the last shot in a string when a 5 will mean a win and a 4 a tie. The more relaxed the rifle shot is, the steadier he tends to be and the more he can concentrate on a gentle trigger squeeze.

127

2. With the left arm in the sling and the left hand in place on the forearm, O'Connor brings up the butt with his right hand. All the action in this picture sequence takes only about two seconds.

3. Loosened grasp shows how sling holds rifle in place, while permitting sufficient flexibility for shots on running game.

If a man misses a standing buck from the sitting position up to 250 yd., it's not because he couldn't hold properly but because he yanked his shot. Really wild shots always come from a yank. Sometimes, of course, a shot may "get away" from a shooter; that's because the rifle goes off when the squeeze is in progress but not at the precise moment the shooter wants it to. Such a shot hits out of the black on the target range, or out of the vital area on game, but the deviation won't be very wide. The lad who misses his game by feet or who knocks out 3's and 2's on a target or misses it completely does so *not* because he cannot hold steady but because he is yanking the trigger. Under any conditions, it must always be squeezed gently. A good rifleman may squeeze it *fast,* but he squeezes it, never yanks it!

Years ago another citizen and I were doing some revolver shooting. I was pretty sour. I protested that I couldn't hold the lousy roscoe steady. "That's not the trouble," quoth my companion. "You're yanking the trigger, trying to catch the 10's as they go by. You can't shoot a handgun like that. You're jerking the whole thing."

Then he demonstrated. He took the revolver and deliberately wobbled it far more than even the poorest holder would. *But he squeezed his shots off.* He didn't get all of them in the black by any means, but he had no wild shots such as I'd been getting. I learned my lesson then and there.

A good gunsling, properly adjusted, is one of the great inventions of the human race, along with fire, the wheel, and good-looking dames. Particularly wonderful is it to the sitting rifleman who wants to polish off a woodchuck perched insolently on a rock at 200 yd. or to nail a fine buck poised for flight high on some lofty ridge way out yonder. Every game shot who takes his shooting seriously owes it to himself to get a good sling, then learn how to adjust it and use it. And never forget that a sling takes the curse off toting a heavy rifle, which otherwise is one of the most awkward burdens known to man. You couldn't run fast enough to present me with a rifle to which a sling could not be attached, even if said rifle were done up in $20 bills.

Best type of sling for the hunter is the one-piece Whelen type, ⅞ in. wide. It's much better for our purposes than the 1¼-in. two-piece military and target sling. Normally, the front swivel should be about 15 in. forward of the center of the trigger. Short-armed men want it farther back, and target shooters who use a low prone position want it farther forward. That's why swivels on target arms are adjustable for position.

The sling can be permanently adjusted for use in the sitting position and for carrying. The one-piece sling is a single strip of leather 52 in. long, with a claw hook at one end; holes are punched into the strap to take the hook. The sling also has two keepers and a stout leather lacing.

The whole key to successful adjustment of the sling for the sitting position is the loop, which is formed when the strap is joined by the leather lacing. I place the lacing 18 in. from the base of the swivel or, with Winchester quick-detachable swivels, about 17 in. from where the sling joins the swivel bow. I put the two keepers on the loop; when both are drawn down against the arm, one helps keep the other in place. Total length of the sling for comfortable carrying is determined by the placement of the claw hook. If, for instance, you want to use both hands for climbing and carry the rifle slung over your back, you can move the claw hook into another set of holes.

No sling without a correctly adjusted loop is worth a hoot. Proper adjustment can be arrived at only by experiment. If the loop is too short or too long, it loses its value and introduces shakes and tremors.

The so-called "hasty" sling, by the way, is a snare and a delusion. After years of solitary, melancholy brooding and endless experiments, I am convinced that the use of the hasty sling is a waste of time and a handicap to the shooter.

The pictures illustrating this article show you how to get into the Whelen-type sling and use it in the sitting position. Except for prone with tight sling, or prone with the fore-end of the rifle resting on some object, this is the steadiest of hunting positions and the easiest to shoot accurately from.

The rough-and-ready "practical" hunter should not sneer at it as belonging only on the target range. It's a wonderfully effective position for the game shot, one that enables him to place his bullets humanely on big game and to knock off varmints at long ranges when he cannot lie prone.

Last summer George Pfeffer, Doc Braddock, and I were walking across a field of high grass headed for a big canyon full of rockchucks when George got his binoculars on a patriarchal chuck perched on a rock, gleaming russet against the blue sky, and a good 300 yd. away. I was nominated to take the shot. I dropped to the sit, but since I did not get into the sling I could not hold the .220 Swift's 10X Unertl scope steadily enough on the small mark. I fired as the crosshairs swung by the chuck and apparently missed by so much that the crack of the bullet didn't bother him.

I paused then, slipped my arm into the loop of the sling, and pulled up the keepers. The difference was astonishing. With the magnificent definition of that big scope I could hold right on the chuck's head to allow for a little bullet drop. As I put the last fraction of an ounce of pressure on the trigger, the crosshairs were glued momentarily on the chuck's head. The bullet landed right in his chest and he flattened.

Best group I ever shot on a big-game animal from the sitting position with a tight sling was on a grizzly at about 200 yd. with a .30/06 and 180-gr. bullet. First shot caught him standing, second and third when he was trying to get out of the open and into the timber, fourth when he was lying on the ground — the last shot was for luck. All four shots could be covered by the palm of the hand. Now, luck played a big part in that shooting, but the tight sling in a good sitting position had a lot to do with it, too. In case that's a hard one to take, I had a witness, Field Johnson of Champagne, Yukon Territory.

The sitting position, then, is one to cultivate, both with and without sling, if you aspire to be a good game shot. If you practice it, you'll be rewarded by shots that will warm your heart and by trophies you couldn't otherwise have got.

It's the ace of the hunting positions!

CHAPTER XV

Hot Rifles for Varmints

Development of the high-powered
twenty-twos has revolutionized
the rifleman's sport

BY JACK O'CONNOR

O NE of the most revolutionary and most influential cartridges ever developed in the United States is the .22 Hornet. No young shooter can possibly realize the fuss that the introduction of the Hornet kicked up, but broken-down old rifle nuts like me are well aware of the revolution started by those wild-eyed radicals at Winchester when they put the .22 Hornet cartridge on the market in the early '30's.

Before the Hornet came out, a lot of casual varmint-shooting was done with the .22 Long Rifle cartridge, which, not long before, had been given a brass case and stepped up about 200 foot seconds in velocity to its present high-speed form. But at that time, the most popular factory center-fire varmint cartridge was probably the .25/20, with the more hep riflemen handloading 93-gr. Luger bullets and 115-gr. .32/20 bullets in the .30/06 for varmints. With its loud report, considerable recoil, and only so-so accuracy with light bullets in a 1-10 twist, the .30/06 just isn't a very good varmint cartridge.

Then the Hornet came along. It was based on the case of the old Winchester .22 W.C.F. — a cartridge then almost dead and practically forgotten — and souped up with new smokeless powders, non-corrosive primers, and jacketed bullets. Winchester was the first in the field with Hornet cartridges, but I believe Savage broke the tape with the first factory-made rifle. Then Winchester chambered its Model 54 for the Hornet. By some hook or crook, I managed to acquire a Model 54, along with a target-type scope of about 3X, and went out on a prairie-dog hunt. With me was a very good shot who used an accurate .22 rimfire rifle with a similar scope. I found out a couple of things that day: First, that a Hornet with a 3X scope is better on varmints than any .22 rimfire ever made, and second, that a Hornet is underscoped with a 3X.

The hot-shot .22's (l. to r.): .22 Hornet, grandaddy of all the modern center-fire .22's; "blown out" K-Hornet; .218 Bee; Mashburn Bee; the .222 Remington; .219 Zipper; blown-out Improved Zipper; and .220 Swift.

My companion consistently killed prairie dogs to about 85 yd. I killed almost all I shot at to about 125 yd. Beyond that distance, the Hornet still had plenty of punch and a sufficiently flat trajectory, but if a pairie dog was partly concealed by grass, lying flat, or otherwise not in good clear view, the scope did not define it well enough for me to be sure of hitting it.

Sighted in as it was, to put its bullets 1 in. above line of scope sight

133

at 100 yd., my Hornet put them about 1 in. low at 150, thus making hits possible on small critters at that distance.

Compared with the Hornet, a .22 Long Rifle high-speed bullet is only about an 85-yd. performer, judging by the same 1-in. rise and fall from line of sight. The top of the curve is at 50 yd. At 75, the bullet is striking at point of aim, and at about 85 it is 1 in. low. At 100 yd. it is 3 in. low, at 125 it is 7 in. low, and at 150 it is 15 in. low. Many men sight in their plinking rifles at 50 yd., and their bullets land 27 in. low at 150.

With the Hornet's point-blank range of 150 yd. (in a properly sighted rifle) and accuracy that keeps all well-held shots in a 2½ to 3-in. circle at that distance *on a still day,* the varmint hunters really had themselves a tool.

Later I experimented with other scopes. I moved to an area where there were plenty of jackrabbits but no prairie dogs. I tried an 8X and then a 6X target model, but finally settled for a 4X hunting-type scope. The 8X, I found, added little or nothing to the effective range I had with the 4X, and I decided that the definition of a good 4X will get just about all there is out of a Hornet. Trajectory takes a dive out beyond 150 yd., and in addition the light, blunt bullets are very wind-sensitive.

On the other hand, there used to be a lot of unjustified criticism that Hornet rifles changed their points of impact from week to week and from day to day. But that doesn't happen if the barrel and action are well bedded in the stock. My Model 54 would hold its point of impact month after month. What fooled the boys was wind drift, not any inherent defect in their rifles. The Hornet was, and still is, a fine varmint cartridge. Its mild report makes it particularly valuable in settled areas, where landowners are afraid of rifles that make more noise, and will shoo away their users. Thus a Winchester Model 70 or Model 43, or a Savage Model 342, plus a good 4X scope, make a fine Hornet outfit for beginners in settled farming country where small-varmint ranges run to about 125-150 yd. The Finnish-made Sako L-46 and the Czech Z-B Mausers are also available in .22 Hornet as well as in .218 Bee.

The introduction of the Hornet gave the boys ideas and inspired a flood of wildcats that is still in full tide. One of the first was the .22/3000 Lovell, which was simply the old .25/20 single-shot case

134

necked to .22. The .22/3000 was later blown out or fire-formed to the 2-R Lovell shape — also known as the R-2 — and another wildcat was born. With 50-gr. bullets, 2-R velocities ran from 3,000 to 3,150. It was a flatter-shooting cartridge than the Hornet, jumping the sure-hitting range by 50 or 75 yd. and making an 8X scope a good accessory.

I used to sight in a heavy-barreled 2-R to put a bullet on point of aim at 200 yd. Then a bullet would rise about 1½ in. at 150 yd. and drop 1½ in. at around 225. With some Arkansas elevation in my holding, I now and then hit jacks at close to 300 yd.

The .22 Hornet is a good varmint rifle in settled areas. Above is an imported model—the Z-B Mauser. Text compares virtues of the .22 Center-fire cartridges.

The 2-R, with some of the recommended loads, is a very hot cartridge. And even the little Hornet produces pressures of around 42,000 pounds per square inch — as much as the .30/40 Krag's. Ballistically the .222 Remington, which we'll talk about later, is almost a dead ringer for the 2-R, and is, I believe, a better-balanced cartridge.

The next factory cartridge in the .22 hot-shot class was the .218 Bee, which Winchester brought out in a light lever-action rifle, a revision of the old Model 1892 that was titled the Model 65. The Bee moves a 46-gr. bullet at 2,860 foot seconds. Inherently it is just as accurate as the Hornet, as well as flatter-shooting and easier to reload. The Model 65, however, was by no means an ideal varmint rifle. It

135

ejected cases straight up, so that its scope had to be offset a bit. It did not deliver quite as good accuracy with the Bee cartridge as the Model 70 did with the Hornet. The Model 65 has been discontinued; now the only American factory rifle made for the Bee is the Winchester Model 43. I would prefer it to the Hornet, particularly if I were going to reload for it.

From the Hornet and the Bee other wildcats have been developed, in each case by fire-forming or blowing out their cases in rechambered rifles. One is the K-Hornet pioneered by Lysle D. Kilbourn, of Whitesboro, N. Y. Another is the Mashburn Bee, a development of the Mashburn Arms Co., Oklahoma City, Okla. Both cases take larger amounts of slower-burning powders to produce higher velocities (and, I believe, higher pressures) than their prototypes.

An interesting factory .22 center-fire cartridge that has suffered a fate worse than death is the .219 Zipper. It is the old .25/35 case shortened and necked to .22. Pressures are kept low so the cartridge can be safely used in the Model 64 lever-action rifle; muzzle velocity is 3,050 foot seconds with a 56-gr. bullet — about the same as that of the old 2-R and the new .222, with their much smaller cases. The Model 64 in .219 had a long, whippy barrel and the lever action did not lock the cases up tight at the head. The result was only so-so accuracy. Besides that, the rifle was a pretty sad platform to put a scope on. It wasn't accurate enough for varmints or deadly enough for deer. Right away the Zipper *cartridge* got a bad reputation. It was, critics said, poorly designed. Actually, if you have a good single-shot action and a heavy barrel, it is a very accurate cartridge and a pleasant one to shoot. Like the Hornet and the Bee, it has been blown out to form another wildcat, and this "Improved Zipper" is a fine cartridge, not too far behind the .220 Swift and the wildcat .22/.250 (.250/3000 necked to .22).

At present no factory rifle is made for the .219 Zipper. The cartridge is fairly popular with custom makers, however, and each year they build many rifles for it around ancient Remington-Hepburn, Winchester High Side Wall, and Sharps-Borchardt actions.

Of all the factory .22 hot shots, though, the ace is the famous .220 Swift, which is almost as radical a departure among varmint cartridges as the atomic bomb is among weapons of war. In one jump it shot muzzle velocities up from the low 3,000's to the low 4,000's

— 1,000 foot seconds at one crack. And this was done by the conservative Winchester factory! As commercially loaded today, the .220 Swift drives a 48-gr. bullet at a velocity of 4,140.

With it, most varmint shooters suddenly became overgunned. Here was a cartridge so flat-shooting that if you sighted it to put the bullet at point of aim at 250 yd., it rose only 2 in. above the line of scope sight at 150 yd. and fell only 2 in. below it at 300. Here also was a cartridge that, in a good rifle, would shoot into a minute of angle. The average Swift was, is, and always has been the most accurate of factory rifles, both in the Winchester Model 54 and its successor, the Model 70. The varmint hunter with a Swift in his dukes is fresh out of alibis. If he doesn't make a hit on a still day it's because he didn't hold right or because he yanked the trigger.

This lad, using a Model 43 Winchester Hornet and a 5X Weaver K-V scope, is lining up a rockchuck below him in a canyon.

A Swift is wasted on a poor rifleman. And *nobody* can get the full value out of one with anything less than the finest target-type scope of 10X or even 12X. Using a Swift with a 4X or 6X scope is like spending heavy sugar for a sports car that will do 100 miles an hour and then putting a governor on it to keep speed down to 35.

The expert who likes to knock over varmints at long range and is willing to shell out for a scope of great definition cannot go wrong on a Swift. For him I know of no greater bargain than the standard-grade Winchester Model 70 in .220. I have one that was taken right out of the rack and not specially selected. I found that it did its best work after I put a paper shim back of the fore-end and backed out, by a half turn, the screw that ties the barrel to the fore-end.

I used that rifle some time ago with a Unertl 10X Ultra Varmint scope and a lace-on-cheek pad to raise the comb, and it really reached out and snagged them! I believe the best shot I made all season with it was at a chuck that was peeking at me over a rock about 200 yd. away. Only the top of his head above the eyes was showing. I knew the bullet was striking about 1 in. high at that distance, so I held the intersection of the crosshairs slightly into the rock below the chuck's head. When I pressed the trigger, the top of his head flew 50 ft. into the air. About 50 percent of the credit for that shot went to the very accurate rifle, the other 50 percent to the wonderful definition of the big Unertl scope. No matter how accurate a rifle is, no one can hit unless he can see what he's shooting at — and not only see it but see it well.

When the Swift first came out it was widely praised — and widely damned. Some said it was a deadly big-game cartridge on animals up to and including moose. Others swore you couldn't kill even a little white-tail deer with one. It was supposed to be tough on barrels and hard to reload.

Well, a lot of big game, including moose, *has* been killed with the Swift, but it isn't a big-game cartridge and was never intended to be. When the Swift was still spot news, a hunter took one into northwest Sonora, Mexico, and killed two big rams with it at about 200 yd., hitting both through the lungs. They simply sank down, stone dead. About the same time I saw a Swift user take a pop at a big desert mule deer. The bullet hit too far back but the buck went down. We had to cross a canyon to reach the spot, and when he did we found the contents of the stomach scattered all over but the buck gone. We couldn't trail him because it was getting dark.

On another occasion I saw a well-hit buck get away because the bullet went to pieces too fast. Shooting big game with a Swift is over-matching a fine varmint cartridge — simply a stunt.

138

It's true that the Swift is tough on barrels because of high pressures and high bullet velocity. So is the .300 Magnum and, to a lesser extent, the .270. The first Swift barrels were made, I believe, of nickel steel. They washed out quickly where the rifling begins; often a barrel would be shot out in 1,000 rounds. I believe that Winchester then switched, for a time, to chrome-molybdenum, and now uses a very hard and erosion-resistant rustless steel with a high chrome content. I have shot my own Swift around 700 rounds and can discern no sign of erosion or falling off in accuracy.

Many a custom .219 Zipper has been built around the old Winchester High Side Wall single-shot action.

The Swift was also criticized as being difficult to reload. To get good accuracy one presumably had to load to maximum. Cases stretched, necks thickened. They had to be trimmed and reamed.

Seems to me that these early Swift users got into trouble by operating their rifles at full throttle all the time, like a man who never drove his automobile at less than 80 miles an hour. A Swift will shoot just as well — about as flat — with a little less powder, and it will last a lot longer.

In my own Swift I have been using 37.5 gr. of No. 4064 powder with 55-gr. Sierra or Sisk .224 bullets. Day after day that load lands in 2 in. at 200 yd. Cases lengthen and thicken no more than do .270 cases fired with equally hot loads. I have killed a large number of rockchucks with the Swift at 300 yd., and a few at 400. This ordinary run-of-the-factory Swift, with its fine 10X Unertl scope, is the best .22 long-range chuck rifle I've ever had.

Like the other factory .22 hot shots, the Swift case has also been re-shaped by experimenters. Their theory is that a sharper shoulder and less body taper promote better powder combustion, with less length-

For very long ranges, O'Connor likes the flat-shooting .220 Swift and a powerful glass like the 10X Unertl Ultra Varmint.

ening and thickening of the neck. The .220 Weatherby Rocket boosts Swift velocities somewhat, moving a 55-gr. bullet at 4,100 foot seconds with 44 gr. of No. 4064. I have never used this or any of the other blown-out Swifts.

When Remington decided to make a bid for the hot-shot .22 trade, it designed an entirely new cartridge — the .222 Remington — to be used in the short-action Remington Model 722 rifle. The case was designed from scratch, a small rimless job that looks a bit like a minia-ture .250/3000. In performance, powder capacity, and range, the .222

140

is in an intermediate zone between cartridges of the Hornet-Bee class and those of the Swift class. Ballistically it is almost a match for the dying 2-R variety of the .22/3000 Lovell — and with a lot less pressure. Handloaded with 21 gr. of No. 4198, it will move a 55-gr. bullet at 3,100 foot seconds, and at approximately 3,000 with 20 gr. Apparently it is a very accurate cartridge in Remington Model 722 rifles and in Winchester Model 70 Hornets that have been rechambered and altered to .222 by custom gunsmiths. I know of at least one bench-rest competition that was won by a chap with a Model 722 and handloaded .222 ammunition.

So there's the line-up of the factory-made .22 center-fire hot shots. How shall we choose among them?

The man who wants a usable varmint rifle at the lowest cost and is not ambitious to pluck his game off at extreme ranges is very well fixed up with a Winchester Model 43 or Savage Model 342 in .22 Hornet or .218 Bee. A 4X scope of good definition, like the Weaver K-4, will help him get out of his cartridge about everything that's in it, and the price of the whole outfit is not too high. With a rifle of either caliber, a good rifleman is definitely underscoped with anything less than a 4X and undoubtedly overscoped with anything over 6X. Each cartridge is a good bet in areas where a loud report would get a farmer's hackles up or make livestock jittery. Applying the criterion of a maximum trajectory spread of 2 in.—1 in. above line of aim, and 1 in. below — we can rate the Hornet and Bee as 150 to 175-yd. cartridges.

For the chap who wants more range, somewhat flatter trajectory, and better wind-bucking ability, the Remington .222 is a good bet. And so is a custom-made single-shot rifle chambered for the .219 Zipper or Improved Zipper. Either is a 200 or 225-yd. rifle, and that range calls for a scope of at least 6X, possibly 8X. Such an outfit is more expensive, of course, than a Hornet or Bee combination.

Lads who like to reach out 300 yd. or more for a chuck can do no better than latch onto a Swift. If they shoot sitting game (chucks, hawks, crows) they want the finest 10 or 12X scope they can find, because precise long-range shooting at small marks calls for all the definition a man can get.

If, however, they want a combination rifle for small, sitting varmints plus the larger, moving ones like bobcats, coyotes, and galloping jackrabbits, they'd better get one of the 6X hunting-type scopes, such as the Stith Bear Cub, Weaver K-6, Unertl Condor, or the fine 6X Hensoldt now being imported from Germany. Because of their small fields, the high-power target scopes are utterly worthless on running game. That criterion of a 2-in. trajectory spread makes the Swift a 300-yd. varmint rifle. With a good Swift and a good scope *on a still day,* hits on small marks at 400 yd. are not at all impossible.

So take your pick. Your choice depends on what you want to shoot, where you want to shoot, and how far you want to shoot. It also depends on the amount of lettuce in your pocketbook.

CHAPTER XVI

Rifles for Woods Hunting

The modern high-velocity cartridges with light bullets have their limitations in deer hunting

BY JACK O'CONNOR

T ENDENCY these days is all toward high-velocity, flat-shooting cartridges with fairly light bullets. Such cartridges are the business for plains and mountain shooting, and I have done my share to promote them. Because they tend to run pressures up, they are generally fired from bolt-action rifles, and often these muskets weigh from 9 to 10 lb. after the eager hunter has put a scope on them. Their trajectory is as flat as a stretched string and the good ones will drop all their shots into the crown of a hat at 300 yd.

Many a hunter goes forth with such a rifle to hunt white-tail deer and black bear in the heavily wooded East. From my correspondence I'd guess that thousands of Pennsylvania and Michigan deer hunters carry the .30/06 with the 150-gr. bullet or the .270 with the 130-gr. bullet. Not a few of them have 4X scopes on their rifles.

There isn't any doubt that if they make a solid body hit with either bullet the buck will usually go down. If he doesn't die immediately he generally stays down long enough for a finishing shot. Both cartridges are decided killers and most of the bolt-action rifles in which they are shot are very accurate. But does the hunter need all this power, all this accuracy, all this flat-trajectory in the woods? I doubt it.

Quite a few hep riflemen who like a spot of varmint shooting use their .30/06's and .270's in the summer on chucks and in the fall on deer. That's O.K., as long as they do it with their eyes open. Others use the .257 or the .250/3000 as a combination deer-and-chuck rifle. Both cartridges produce top accuracy. Both have adequate power for deer. Either is a pretty fair compromise for varmints and game.

But are all these rifles ideal for the woods? Again, I doubt it.

In mountainous Pennsylvania many smart hunters who are also rifle nuts, accuracy fiends, and crack shots find a seat on a point overlooking good deer country. They arm themselves with .30/06's, .270's, .300 Magnums, or one of the fancier ultrahigh-velocity wildcats with 4X or 6X scopes.

They have good binoculars to locate deer and to distinguish bucks from does. They scan the open spots and the thin places on hillsides, and when a suitable deer shows up they pour it on. They tell me 300-yd. kills are common, and it is by no means unknown for a shrewd rifleman to polish off a buck at 400 yd. and over.

Not long ago a hunter told me that he always chooses a particular rocky point for his hunting. From it he can look down over a wide area. He simply sits there and lets other hunters move the deer to him.

In the winter he does small-bore target shooting indoors, and in the summer he shoots chucks. He says he's generally pretty well on the beam. His usual deer medicine, he said, is a Winchester Model 70 in .300 Magnum with a 6X scope. But a couple of times he has killed bucks with a heavy-barreled .25/06 wildcat chuck rifle having a 10X target scope.

Such hunters may do their shooting in the wooded East but they are by no means typical white-tail hunters. Actually they are mountain hunters using mountain rifles. Our run-of-the-mine deerslayer needs no such equipment. He's much better off with a light rifle with fast action and fast sights, one that moves a fairly heavy bullet at moderate velocity and with moderate recoil. He has no need of ultrahigh velocity or flat trajectory, for he doesn't knock his bucks off at 300 yd., but usually at less than 100.

Neither does he have any use for the hairsplitting accuracy that enables a rifleman to pick a chuck off a rock at 300 yd., because for the ranges at which most forest game is shot, a rifle that will group into 3 in. — or even 4 in. — at 100 yd. is plenty accurate. Most forest game is shot from the offhand position, and the man who can stand on his hind legs and keep his bullets in a 6-in. circle at 100 yd. is a very good shot.

Our woods hunter, then, usually shoots at fairly close range, at a large mark, probably moving, and he shoots on his hind legs. That holds true whether he's a stillhunter, a driver, or a stander. Don't let

O'Connor's Marlin carbine in .35 Remington is handy in brush.

anyone tell you that such shooting is easy. I have missed a higher percentage of bucks with snapshots at short range in heavy cover than I have across open canyons at much greater distances.

Very often our woods hunter has to shoot through brush, and then no poorer missile can be imagined than a light, sharp-pointed, high-velocity bullet. I can remember many occasions when I was unable to get such bullets through heavy cover to the game. Once I was still-hunting moose, carrying a .270 loaded with the old 130-gr. sharp-point Winchester pointed-expanding bullet. I jumped a big bull out of his bed, and the first look I got at him was through a tangle of dead spruce limbs and twigs that were hanging from the lower part of a tree.

I could see the bull's great dark bulk moving behind all those botanical specimens, and I fired when the crosshairs were right on the spot where his shoulders ought to be. Mind you, this bull was not over 30 yd. from me — about 15 yd. on the far side of the tree — and was as large as a big horse. When I fired, twigs, limbs, and bark flew everywhere, but the moose went on. I worked the bolt as he came into the clear for a moment, got the crosshairs against the curve of his paunch at an angle that would drive the bullet up into his lungs, and shot, but the moose went on and out of sight.

I wondered how I could possibly miss a mark as large as the side of a woodshed at 40 yd. or thereabouts. Then I took up his track. He was down in the high willows of a little swamp not over 50 yd. from where he'd been hit by my second bullet. The shot I'd taken in the clear was right where I'd called it, but my first had never touched him.

Another time I was hunting in Mexico with a .30/06. Returning after a fruitless days' hunt I saw a movement on the other side of an ironwood tree about 75 yd. away. It was a big buck deer browsing. I could see him quite plainly despite the intervening foliage, so I decided to take a crack at him. I dropped to one knee and squeezed off a shot. The 150-gr. bullet never reached him. Instead it cut off a limb as cleanly as an ax, and the fork fell right over the deer's shoulders. You should have seen that buck take off. He made Santa Claus's reindeer look earthbound, and I couldn't shoot again for laughing.

Some years ago I spent several afternoons shooting at a target — the outline of a deer — through heavy brush with rifles of different calibers and with different weights of bullets. I found that the higher the bullet velocity, the sharper the point, the thinner the jacket, the lighter the weight, the greater the deflection. I also found that the farther the deer was away from the deflecting brush or limbs, the less liable he was to get hit.

My experiments indicated that behind even thin brush a deer is pretty safe if someone is shooting a .220 Swift, and fairly safe even if the hunter is using the 130-gr. bullet in the .270 or the 150-gr. bullet in the .30/06. But the 150-gr. round-nose .270 bullet gave me a much better chance of hitting. Likewise with the 180-gr. .30/06 round-nose bullets. The 100-gr. .250/3000 bullet was better than the 87-gr., but neither was too good. And in the .257 the 117-gr. was superior to the 100-gr.

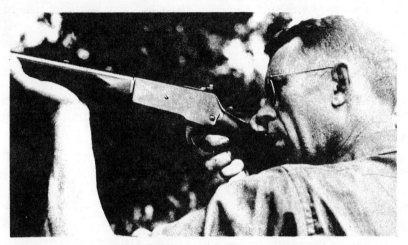

Winchester's lever-action Model 71 and the .348 Winchester cartridge make a powerful combination in timber even on game the size of moose or grizzly bears.

I concluded, too, that the rotational speed of the bullet was apparently responsible for a good deal of the deflection, with the bullet spinning away from the surface it touched just as a billiard ball with a lot of English on it spins away from the cushion or from another ball.

Next I loaded a .220 Swift with some 50-gr. spire-point bullets and shot at my 3x4-ft. deer target, and rarely did I find one except in fragments. Even the big 300-gr. Silvertip bullet in .375 caliber showed plenty of deflection from line of aim; and many .35 Remington 200-gr. bullets reached the target intact but keyholed, or hit on their sides.

Thousands of deer are killed annually through the brush, but if my findings are correct, the man who misses a deer when shooting through cover has an ironclad alibi.

The best missile for getting through obstructions in a straight line is, I discovered, the 12 gauge shotgun slug. It is heavy, massive, slow-moving, and it spins very slowly if at all. (It flies point on only because it is heavier in the front end — like a sock with sand in the toe.) All of which brings up the subject of well-meaning legislators who permit the use of shotgun slugs on deer in populated areas but outlaw high-velocity rifles because of their "great range." To make things really safe, they'd arm all their hunters with .220 Swifts, whose bullets go to pieces immediately upon striking brush. The shotgun with slugs is the most dangerous weapon I can think of in thickly populated areas. Buckshot is something else again, but I still believe the Swift would be safer.

Since the bullet deflects at an angle, the farther the deer is from the obstruction the safer he is. If he is 6 ft. behind the brush he is liable to be hit; if he is 20 ft. away he is pretty safe.

Once one of my sons and I were hunting white-tails when I found, with my binoculars, a sweet buck lying down below us about 75 yd. away. He was in really heavy cover and I never in the world would have found him with the naked eye. First I saw an ear flick. Then I made out antlers and finally (and very vaguely) the outline of his back. The kid's first shot with the 100-gr. Silvertip bullet from his .257 struck a twig about halfway to the buck and was deflected just enough to go over the buck's back. The second shot apparently got through a gap and took the deer right behind the shoulder.

Now, one often hears that a wounded white-tail *always* runs with his tail between his legs. I was watching this buck with the glass as he ran through the brushy basin and came out on an open ridge. His tail was flying like a banner in the wind.

The kid missed a couple of running shots but just as the deer disappeared over the skyline, his tail suddenly dropped and his legs turned to rubber. I knew we'd find him a few yards beyond the crest — and we did. Back at the spot where he'd been bedded, I showed the lad hair and a fan of blood where the second Silvertip had gone right through the buck.

The old .30/30 cartridge with the 170-gr. bullet at 2,200 foot seconds' muzzle velocity is good on deer in wooded country. So are the very similar .32 Special, the .30 and .32 Remington rimless cartridges, the old .303 Savage, and the other ".30/30 class" cartridges. None of

148

them can be depended on to knock a deer off his feet with a poorly placed shot, as more powerful cartridges do, but if a man puts a bullet from any of them into the chest cavity or into the neck close to the vertebrae, he has himself a piece of meat. The old .30/40 with the 220-gr. bullet is also excellent.

Aces among woods cartridges, though, are the .35 Remington, .300 Savage, and .348 Winchester. With the 200-gr. bullets of the .35 and the .348 and the 180-gr. of the .300, the deer hunter gets good penetration, good brush-bucking, and a lot of knockdown power. You need it today in areas where the hunter must get his tag on a buck quickly before someone else claims it, and so these more powerful cartridges are a good idea. The 200-gr. flat-point .348 bullet is one of the best brush bullets ever designed and, as far as I could tell from my tests, the best brush bullet made today.

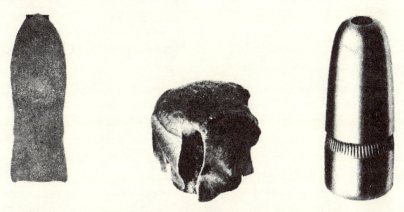

Above is a round-nosed Remington bullet shown in section, mushroomed, and whole. This type, fired at moderate velocity gets through brush better than a light spitzer bullet moving at high velocity but more easily deflected.

Excellently stocked and fast-handling woods rifles in current production are the Winchester Models 64 and 71, Marlin Model 36, Remington Model 760, and Savage Model 99's. They have fast actions, handle fast, and are available in good woods calibers.

The man who wants to hunt deer in the woods with a bolt-action rifle can do so, and I'll have to admit that my own all-time favorite brush rifle was a 7-lb. Mauser 7 mm. with a very straight stock and a Lyman 1-A cocking-piece sight. But lever-actions and pumps are preferable because they let you get off a second shot in jig time if your first bullet doesn't get through the brush.

The .270 user should do his woods hunting with the 150-gr. soft-point bullet; the .30/06 user with the 180-gr. soft-point. Best 7 mm. bullet for woods use is the standard 175-gr. soft-point; best .257 bullet, the 117-gr. I'll undoubtedly be hanged for this, but I think the best and most reliable deer bullets for short range are the old-fashioned soft-points with relatively thin jackets and plenty of penetration on white-tails with any reasonable bullet. With the .270's 130-gr. bullet I have shot through three-fourths the length of a deer.

But I've had a good deal of trouble with bullets that opened up *too* slowly. One lot of .257 controlled-expanding 100-gr. bullets I used on a month's hunt in Mexico were really turkeys. They'd go right through deer broadside with practically no expansion, and for that reason I chased wounded deer all over northern Mexico.

With a fancy .30/06 bullet I once shot clear through a big ram from rump to brisket. I didn't do him any good — but I didn't knock him over in his tracks either.

Darndest thing I ever saw, though, happened with a controlled-expanding .30/30 bullet. An Arizona antelope hunter took a pop at a buck running away. The bullet hit the animal between the hams and went clean through the body cavity, up the neck, and out the forehead between the horns. The buck died, of course, but if our hunter had hit it broadside he wouldn't have known it.

Best iron sight for the woods rifle is a peep; using it, the hunter does not have a tendency to shoot high, as he would with open sights. The larger the aperture, the faster and better the sight. And the closer the aperture is to the eye (within reason) the faster it is and the more one can see through it. Fastest of all iron sights are the old Lyman and Marble tang and cocking-piece sights. But if you use one, be sure it is mounted far enough from the eye so that it won't drive back in recoil and injure the eye. Front sight should be a conspicuous gold bead — 3/32 or even 1/16 in.

Western hunters have taken to scope sights with great enthusiasm. Although more and more woods hunters are using scopes, the glass sight is relatively much less popular in the East than in the West. "Why should I use a scope?" the Eastern hunter asks. "My shots are at short range."

Why, indeed, my good fellow? Because the scope — of suitable power, low mounting, and with proper eye relief — is a tremendously fast sight. Still more important, it is so easy to *see* with. With a good scope the hunter can apparently look right through brush and plainly see a deer that otherwise would be but a gray-brown blur. Since he can distinctly see intervening limbs and brush he can find an opening and shoot through it without having a deflected bullet.

He can tell a buck from a doe, and a hunter from a deer. The day before I wrote this I was talking to a friend whose son had shot and killed another friend of mine whom he mistook for an elk in heavy cover. I had hunted with them a few days earlier.

"Never again," my friend told me, "will my boy or I hunt without a scope. If we'd had scope-sighted rifles that day, we'd have known instantly that what we saw was a man, not an elk."

Best scope for the woods is one of from 2X to 2¾X — the Weaver K-2.5, the Lyman Alaskan, the Stith 2¾X Bear Cub, the Texan, the 2¾X Unertl, a Leupold, etc. Since it's easy to lose a crosshair in poor light against dead leaves and twigs, I'd select a flat-topped post or a large, conspicuous dot subtending 4 or 6 in. at 100 yd.

Because the deer woods are often wet with rain or snow, I like the scope mounted on a deer rifle with a quick-detachable mount. Then, in a pinch, iron sights of some sort can be used. Jaeger, Mykrom, and Echo mounts are good. So is the novel Packmayr Lo-Swing. An old time-tried favorite in this category, and one which I have used for many years, is the Griffin & Howe.

While I'm at it, I am going to toss an idea to you readers and before you start fighting over it, I'll duck so I won't get hit. This is it: I do not think there is any *ideal* brush cartridge for deer and black bears. With the exception of the fine .300 Savage and .348 Winchester, all the standard and wildcat cartridges that have come along in the last 40 years have been ultrahigh-velocity super-dupers for plains and mountain use. Deer cartridges have remained about where they were in the early days of smokeless powder. The .30/30 and its running mates could use a bit more velocity and a bit more bore diameter as well as heavier bullet. The .348 has pretty husky recoil for the once-a-year hunter. The .300 Savage could ideally use a bullet of larger diameter.

So let's take the 7 mm. Mauser case, neck-expand it to .33, and load a 200-gr. bullet in it. Or expand it to .35 and load a 225-gr. bullet. Use a bullet with a flat nose having plenty of lead exposed. Then drive it along at 2,400-2,450 foot seconds. Put the cartridge in an action like the Remington Model 760. Then you'd have something!

Our bullet would get through the brush well. It would open up fast, have a lot of shocking power. If it didn't go through an animal it would leave a substantial hole to leak blood and make trailing easy. Recoil wouldn't be bad, and we'd have trajectory flat enough so we could sight in to get a 2-in. rise above line of sight at 100 yd.; then the bullet would strike only about 2 in. low at 200. Actually that would make a pretty good moose outfit.

To sum up: Our deer rifle for woods and brush is a specialized weapon — and one that has been kept in the shadow of the ultrahigh-velocity hot shots. The man who has a good one, who sights it in properly, and who learns to use it usually brings home the venison.

CHAPTER XVII

Let Deer Come to You

Why wear yourself out on a deer stalk
when you can take it easy — with
better results?

BY CARNES LEE

B Y FAR the biggest portion of deer taken annually in the eastern
half of the United States — probably 80 or 90 percent — are
shot when they walk in to the hunter, not when he deliberately takes
to their track and hunts them down.

Many hunters, trying to carry the hunt to the deer, underestimate
what they are up against. They forget that while a white-tail may
blunder now and then, he can also be about as crafty and cunning
as any game animal ever gets to be.

To begin with, the deer has the advantage of knowing the country
far better than the hunter does. If he's in his home territory — and
he rarely leaves it — there isn't a swamp, runway, thicket, ravine, or
ridge that he's not familiar with, and he knows 'em the way a man
knows the location of each piece of furniture in his living room.

In the second place, the deer's nervous system is instinctively alert
to danger signals to a degree that no human can comprehend. It takes
only the slightest hint of something suspicious in the neighborhood
to put a buck on guard. The breaking of a dry stick or the crackle of
dead leaves underfoot, the scrape of clothing against brush, the crunch
of thin ice in a frozen swamp, a word spoken in an undertone, the
merest trace of man smell — any of these is ample warning.

153

As for his natural alarm system, it's too well known to require much discussion. He can hear you a great deal farther than you can hear him, smell you at distances that are almost incredible, and see you farther and more quickly than you'd expect him to — especially if you move or place yourself in silhouette against sky or snow.

All of which means that if you try to stalk him in the brushy country where he is most likely to be found there's a good chance he will discover your presence before you discover his — unless you are extra careful or extra lucky or both. And when he spots you, you may as well look for another deer.

The advantages of letting him come to you are obvious. That way, if any noise is made the deer will make it. Since you'll be standing still while he is moving you can be reasonably sure of seeing him before he sees you. And if you gauge the wind direction in relation to likely runways, an approaching deer probably won't get your scent.

Now, I'm not belittling stillhunting. It happens to be my favorite method. I don't care much about waiting on a stand while a drive tries to send a buck my way. And my patience in runway watching on a cold November morning is decidedly limited. So stillhunting is about all that's left for me.

There are ways, however, to give a deer a chance to come to you even when you're stillhunting.

The basic requirements are to move slowly and quietly. Especially slowly. The stillhunter who sets out to see a lot of country may have a good time but he is not likely to hang up a deer. No better advice was ever given than the time-honored injunction of the deer woods: "Take one step and stand still two."

The method I like best is to combine runway watching and still-hunting, taking both in alternate small doses. Normally I take a stand on a runway at daybreak, or a little before, and sit until my teeth begin to chatter — or, if the weather is mild, until I get bored beyond endurance. In either case that means not less than twenty minutes or more than a couple of hours.

When the impulse to move becomes too strong to be denied, I leave the stand and walk until my blood is circulating again, and that takes from fifteen minutes to half an hour. Then I look for another good location and sit down again.

I keep that schedule up pretty continuously throughout the day if the weather permits. Deer are supposed to move only in early morning and late afternoon, lying up in the middle hours. But frequently they ignore that routine, especially in country that's heavily hunted. If there are enough hunters to keep them restless they are as likely to travel at noon as at daybreak. In my case runway watching in the middle of the day has paid off surprisingly often.

Even when I'm on the move, between stands, I give the deer every possible opportunity to come to me. I avoid thick places where I can't get through without noise, frozen pools where I'm sure to break ice, and other hazards. I stop every few yards and I'm in no hurry to get started again. If a deer is coming my way I want to give him ample opportunity to get within range without discovering I'm there. Fairly often he obliges me if I wait long enough.

One fall morning, I left camp half an hour before daylight and walked out to a promising stand I'd located the afternoon before. It was on the side of a ridge above a thick green swamp, at the junction of two runways that came up out of the swamp.

It was a cold, windy morning, with a few stray flakes of snow, and my stand was anything but comfortable. Chills were running up my spine ten minutes after I'd settled myself in the lee of an old stump.

A little after shooting light had arrived, a sleek little doe came along the nearer runway, out of the thick cover of the swamp. At a point directly below me, hardly fifty feet away, she stopped to feed. I was well screened from sight and she hung around for quite a spell, browsing and nibbling and enjoying her breakfast. Every little while she looked back across her shoulder in a way that convinced me there was a buck behind her, somewhere back in the swamp.

That belief helped me to endure the biting wind for a long half-hour after the doe had finally wandered off out of sight. Shaking with cold, I looked at my watch and set myself a stint of another ten minutes. When I looked again, convinced the time was up, I found I still had six minutes to go, so I quit the stand in disgust, and decided to attempt to warm up instead.

To find shelter from the wind I went down through the swamp to an old, brushy logging road that had been cut when the big cedars were taken out thirty years before. A road of that kind is by no means ideal for stillhunting. The hunter who follows it is too much in the open and the cover on each side is too thick for him to see more than a few yards. Virtually his only chance lies in a deer happening to enter or cross the road ahead of him.

But I was more interested just then in protection from the weather than in killing a deer, so I started slowly down the road, hunting into the wind.

I loafed along for half a mile without seeing even a fresh track. By that time I was warm and comfortable, and I decided it was time to do a little more runway watching. At a spot where the road forked, giving me a clear view for fifty or sixty yards in two directions, I scraped snow off a log behind a clump of low evergreens and sat down.

I had made a bit of unavoidable racket in getting myself established, what with gathering the shin-tangle and all, and I'd have bet that for at least five or ten minutes no deer would show up. But a minute or so after I got in position, with my .300 Savage lying across my lap, I happened to glance around at the road behind me, and when I turned back, a fine little buck with a six-point rack was standing in the open just beyond the forks. I'd heard no brush break, had had no warning of any kind. He'd just stepped out of the cedars like a rabbit popping out of a magician's hat and there he was. I anchored him with a shot in the base of the neck, at about forty feet, and he went down without a quiver.

The point is, I could have hunted that deer the rest of the day out there in the thick tangles of the swamp and not seen so much as his flag. Had I kept going, instead of sitting on the log, I'd never have known he was there.

Up in northern Wisconsin early one season I was on a stand at the edge of an abandoned clearing. There had been an orchard there once, and a few of the ancient trees still stood, gnarled and half dead, but bearing a crop of scrubby fruit. An old orchard of that kind, walled in by brush and timber on all sides, is an excellent place to look for deer at the beginning of the season. I knew a big buck had been feeding regularly in this one, mornings and evenings, for more than a month.

I picked a stand at the edge of the brush on one side of the clearing, where half-a-dozen summer runways fanned out between the apple trees. I had the wind in my favor and I figured I was reasonably sure to kill a deer.

156

About fifteen minutes after I got set, and just as it was getting light enough to see both sights, another hunter came into the far side of the clearing. He looked the place over, apparently liked it, and sat down under the low branches of a big spruce tree that stood by itself a few yards out from the timber. His red hunting coat and cap loomed up plainly against the trunk. I was more carefully hidden and, so far as I could tell, he did not know I was there.

Ten minutes later the buck I was awaiting walked into the lower end of the clearing. There had been no shooting in that neighborhood, so he was no more than normally cautious. He came to the edge of the brush, took a long look all around and started up the far side of the old field, 400 yards from me, headed straight for the hunter at the spruce. I sat there — cussing under my breath but grinning in spite of myself — and watched the whole performance like a scene on a movie screen.

That deer should have seen the red cap and coat, but he didn't and strolled on. When I realized I'd get no chance to shoot, I picked up my binoculars for a close-up view of the climax.

The other hunter was no rookie. He didn't get buck fever or make any false moves, but twisted slowly around into a better position for shooting. Then he brought his rifle to his shoulder, covered the deer, and waited until the range closed to less than fifty yards. At his shot the buck wheeled and started straight toward me. But his flag was down and before he had moved five times his length he collapsed in a heap.

I walked over and congratulated the stranger, admired his deer, and moved on to do some still hunting. I had in mind a series of small swamps and hemlock ridges farther to the west. The orchard, I told myself, would be no good for at least three or four hours.

At the top of the next ridge I sat down on a log to think things over and mourn my carelessness.

I was deeply preoccupied when I heard a stick break down toward the foot of the ridge — and saw as handsome a buck as any man ever looked at step out of the cedars. He stopped in a little opening, knee-deep in frost-seared brown brakes, and the morning sun turned his rack into antlers of polished mahogany. He stood with head up and ears cocked forward, alert and watchful, and every hair on his sleek gray body seemed to shine and glisten. I admired him as long as I dared, which wasn't long. His manner indicated plainly that he was uneasy there in the open. I killed him with a spine shot high in the shoulder.

Giving a deer a chance to come to me never paid bigger dividends than it did then — even though my stopping was purely accidental and I had no reason to expect a deer after the commotion in the vicinity.

I still remember the first buck I ever killed. Two of us were still-hunting, moseying along, "taking one step and standing still two." Some other hunters put a buck out of an alder swamp a quarter-mile ahead of us, but we didn't know it. He trotted toward us, blundering into me at the edge of an old burn, and I nailed him with a shot just over the heart.

One point in all this can hardly be overemphasized: Watch the direction of the wind and make sure no ribbon of scent betrays your presence.

Man smell is one danger signal that no deer ever disregards. The stupidest buck in the woods is not going to come within shooting range if he gets a whiff of you in advance.

I know hunters who won't smoke in the deer woods, but I can't go along with their reasoning. A white-tail can smell a man about as far as he can smell tobacco fumes, and of the two he likes the man scent a whole lot less!

Every once in a while, when conditions are right, you may want to try tracking a buck to its bed. Sooner or later, if you're skillful, you may succeed.

But remember that of the two basic methods of hunting white-tails — going after them or letting them come to you — the latter pays off far more frequently. As an old-timer told me many years ago, "You kill a lot more deer settin' than walkin'!"

CHAPTER XVIII

Track that Wounded Deer

Learn to read hoofprints and you'll know, not only where he's going, but whether he has been hit

BY C. P. BARAGER

T RACKING is not a difficult phase of woodcraft. True, it cannot be learned in one day in the woods, or even one year, but the once-a-year hunter can master enough of it to enable him, in most cases, to recover a wounded deer.

When he has fired, the hunter must watch closely for any reaction in the animal's pace. The effortless bounce may change into a sluggish jump. A standing, walking, or trotting animal may start off on a sudden, violent run.

Do not be misled if no blood signs show along the trail. The animal may still be hard hit. Not infrequently a deer that's been shot through the heart will run a couple of hundred yards before dropping dead.

One tip-off of a wounded deer is the fact that it carries its tail tucked in close to its rump. An unharmed animal holds its flag high and above its back. (Occasionally a badly frightened but unhurt buck will carry its tail low for the first few bounds.)

In heavy cover where the game goes out of sight with the first jump — as in the case of my deer — you must rely on trail evidence. But here you can detect a change of pace as readily as if you'd seen the animal take off. Study the sketch for a few minutes and you'll see that the tracks of a walking unwounded buck are placed quite differ-

159

ently from those of an unwounded buck that's running or jumping. But in each case the prints are astride an imaginary line representing the course of travel. There is no weaving from side to side of that line. If you come upon a trail like that you can safely conclude you have missed your shot.

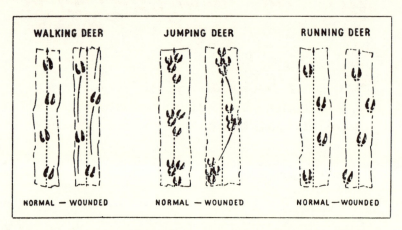

The trail of a wounded animal, walking, running, or jumping, is something else again. The tracks are erratic, veering to and from the imaginary line of progress. Sometimes they are close to the center line, sometimes wide, often varying every second or third pace. In other words, the buck weaves and staggers like a drunken man trying to walk a chalk line. And a practiced eye will disclose that fact from the trail alone.

If the buck is running or jumping, his footprints may be grouped closely, then spread apart.

Tracks showing any irregularity should be followed.

Many hunters assert that wounded deer always run downhill. That statement needs qualification. A wounded deer, like any other wounded animal, tries to reach heavy, concealing cover in which to bed down. In typical deer country, the ridges and higher ground are usually more open; hence a hard-hit animal will travel downhill to denser cover — a swamp, a heavy thicket, or a rank growth of grass. If heavy cover happens to grow above him, the animal will travel uphill instead of down. In seeking a lost trail, always look first in the nearest concealing cover.

Once you have scored a hit, try to determine where the wound has occurred. This will be of considerable value in knowing how long to wait before taking up the trail. A body shot, placed high and behind the lungs, is indicated by blood appearing at a height on any brush which the animal has touched in passing. Its color will be slightly darker than that of blood coming from a wound in the shoulder or other large muscle. A lung shot is betrayed by bright blood flecked with foam. And that usually means the animal will be found dead within a short distance. A broken leg is easily evident from the tracks and from blood dripping directly onto the trail. Dark bloodstains and bits of stomach contents indicate that the animal has been hit through the paunch.

One of the first tracking lessons I learned was how long to wait out wounded game. When the animal has been shot through the shoulders or legs, wait for fifteen minutes before following the trail. As an old woodsman friend of mine would say: "Sit down and smoke a pipe." If the game lies down for a short time the wound will stiffen and the animal will not rise as quickly when approached. A stomach shot should be waited out for a slightly longer time, twenty minutes or so. As a rule it is unwise to wait much longer than half an hour at any time, since the numbing effect of the wound may wear off and the animal may give you considerable chase before a finishing shot can be delivered.

But there are exceptions. In falling rain or snow get on the trail as soon as possible; also if the animal is wounded shortly before dark.

Where tracks are being obliterated by rain or snow, you may keep on the trail by observing an occasional drop of blood and the clear imprint of tracks under any protecting foliage where the deer has passed. Scuffed leaves or bits of fresh-turned earth will guide you across the open stretches.

Sometimes the presence of other deer tracks complicates your task. Then it's important to know the size and shape of the track you are following. How? Well, close examination of deer tracks reveals how hoofprints vary between one animal and another. Every deer has its own individual print. For instance, not one animal in a hundred leaves a perfect print. Even the hoofprints of the same deer vary in conformity. One hoof may be chipped only slightly, while another may be broken off square. Chips and irregularities come from uneven wear and may be present on the inside or the outside of the hoof.

Before starting on a trail, take your knife and notch the exact width and length of the track on a short piece of stick. Use this to check with, from time to time, and keep in mind the peculiarities you have noted in the hoofs. That way you are not likely to be misled by another set of prints. When possible, first measurements should be taken on fairly level ground. A deer's footprint will not vary under an even gait, but uphill going will shorten the prints and downhill going will lengthen them.

Tracking down a wounded deer calls for a great deal of caution. A wounded animal is always nervous and frightened, and unless badly hit is easy to put up. It constantly watches its back trail and is always testing the air currents for sight, sound, or smell of an approaching enemy. The hunter should proceed slowly and watch all cover for any disturbance that might mean game.

When two men are hunting together, one should follow the trail after his partner has stationed himself well ahead. The tracker gives his associate enough time to make a wide circle and get posted, then he devotes all his attention to the trail and works each clump of brush in detail. As deer country usually has openings between the timber growths, the second man should select a stand that commands a clear view and affords an open shot.

Tracking is an art, but not a lost one. Nor is learning it a hopeless proposition. Following the trail of wounded game is much the same as stillhunting. Learn to track and you will not be guilty of leaving a wounded animal to die a lingering death.

CHAPTER XIX

Make Your Decoys Work

Here are tricks that will bring
the ducks in

BY ALLAN H. MURDOCK
SKETCHES BY FRANK HUBBARD

S HOOTING over artificial decoys is perhaps the most popular method of hunting ducks in North America today. The art of decoying is practiced from the Arctic to Mexico and from coast to coast. Yet, in spite of most sportsmen's general familiarity with this method of luring waterfowl within range of their guns, few present-day hunters get the most out of their decoys.

Those who do all their shooting over rigs provided and set out by guides or owners of blinds naturally have little interest in how the "blocks" are displayed on the water. Most duck hunters handle their own rigs — and many fall far short of getting maximum effectiveness out of them because they are content to use mediocre decoys and careless spreads.

Now and again these happy-go-lucky methods of decoying pay off in limit kills, but much more often they are the cause of blank days. As one of the old-timers I learned about duck shooting from once told me, "Some days ducks are dumb as mud, but most days they're smart as paint. On their dumb days they'll decoy to an old derby hat, but on their smart days they won't come to your stool unless it looks and *acts* just like a passel of birds who've found a feeding spot that's so derned good those birds up in the air just can't bear not to be in on it. If you want to kill your fair share of ducks, you'd better figure that every day you shoot is one of the birds' smart days, and set out your stool accordingly."

The art of decoying has three essentials. You must use decoys which look enough like live ducks to fool the most suspicious, gimlet-eyed old drake. You must set them out in the right position relative to your blind and the wind. And the spread must look natural.

Too many duck hunters assume that any fairly reasonable imitation of a live duck will lure waterfowl within shotgun range. In this they are badly mistaken. Ducks and geese are among the wariest of game-birds. To fool them a decoy must be lifelike, both in coloring and shape.

In the old days each town and village in every good duck-shooting district had its stool makers. Many of them were market hunters or guides who knew all about how ducks look and act, and also were homespun artists. The decoys they turned out — at a quarter or at most half a dollar apiece — fooled both ducks and duck hunters at a little distance. Some of these old-time craftsmen achieved their effects by careful attention to detail in carving and painting, others by crude but highly realistic "hatchet sculpturing" and seemingly slapdash splashes of paint. However they turned the trick, their masterpieces had one quality in common — the ducks came to them!

Fine stool makers, however, are now extremely scarce. If you are lucky enough to locate a first-rate professional he'll probably make you blocks as good as any that ever were turned out, but he'll charge you $40 or more a dozen for them.

So now most duck hunters have to be satisfied with factory-made decoys. Some of the cruder mass-production marvels being sold to inexperienced gunners no doubt are responsible for many disappointing hunts. Although most of even the better machine-made blocks are lacking in masterly design and coloration, they are quite natural in appearance and, properly used, bring satisfactory results. Many of them have the advantage of being extremely light — but the best ones are priced so high that they are out of reach of many gunners.

Some of today's finest decoys are made by amateur sportsmen who find off-season enjoyment at their work-benches. Here, of course, their time and labor are paid for by the pleasure they get from doing something they like to do.

164

Whether you buy or make them, get the very best decoys you can — and be sure that they represent the sorts of waterfowl you plan to hunt.

Among deepwater ducks — those which dive for their food — are the canvasback, redhead, and scaup. They all are notably low riders — they float with their tails barely clearing the surface of the water. Almost all divers have much the same feeding and resting habits, and from a distance look much alike. Consequently decoys representing one kind often will work quite well on the rest. For instance, a canvasback set sometimes will draw bluebills (greater scaup) and redheads. However, canvasbacks will come most readily to canvasback blocks — this is due to their larger size and longer necks and bills.

On Chesapeake Bay's famous Susquehanna Flats, where the canvasback is king, practically all the decoys are cans. Farther down the Bay, where much of the shooting is provided by black ducks, redheads, and scaup, blocks representing canvasbacks, redheads, and scaup usually are used in mixed stools. Blackduck decoys seldom are mixed with the diver-duck blocks. They are set, often combined with mallards, in a separate spread which is placed close to shore.

It has been my experience that redheads and bluebills are seldom choosy in selecting their associates. In fact, these two ducks will sometimes come into decoys of the dipper or shallow-water duck class.

Ducks come most readily to those blocks which best simulate the plumage of the season. Remember that the drakes do not assume their full plumage early in the fall. Then your decoy spread should major in hens. (In a pinch, decoys painted dark brown can be used effectively to represent the females of a number of species.) As the season advances, a bit of whiting on their backs will simulate the gray-brown of the "canvas" patch. Finally, late in the season, when you commence to bag drakes that are fully plumaged, is time enough for you to switch to spreads in which drakes predominate.

This seasonable-plumage rule, like all duck-hunting precepts, isn't unbreakable. In fact, in some regions many successful early-season rigs have a majority of drake decoys.

Decoys for marsh or puddle ducks, which include mallards, teal, spoonbills, pintails, and blackies, should be extremely well designed and their colors applied with great care. This is important. Divers sometimes will come to blocks which are a bit crude, but not the wise old mallard or pintail. A black duck will be doubly critical; this bird demands the best imitations, whether they represent its own kind or other sorts — such as the canvasback — with which it sometimes associates.

You'll get more ducks if you have some geese decoys in your outfit, for ducks show special interest in such a set. This is particularly true of black ducks and pintails, but it often works for mallards.

Get the best decoys you possibly can, then, and be sure to have enough. How many you will need depends on where, and what kind of ducks, you are going to hunt.

To be properly rigged for divers, which are mostly found in large flocks on the more open and deeper waters, you should have from three dozen to 120 blocks — and there will be days when you'll wish you had even more. Big rigs are especially prevalent in coastal waters — from 100 to 250 blocks for broadbills on New York's Great South Bay, up to 500 canvasback decoys on the Susquehanna Flats, from 50 to 200 diver-duck stools on lower Chesapeake Bay, and from 150 to 300 canvasback and redhead blocks on Virginia's Back Bay and North Carolina's Currituck Sound.

Practically any seasoned duck hunter will tell you that he never can have too many blocks out when gunning on big water, whether salt or fresh. For late-season work especially, when wintry blasts have sent birds in flocks of 200 or more into your territory, 50 to 75 decoys may not be nearly enough. At such times ducks seem to feel there is safety in numbers, and they will decoy best to a spread big enough to give them a sense of security and companionship.

The number of decoys needed in shallow-water rigs depends mostly on the size of the water. If your blind is on the shore of a large lake or a wide river, the more decoys you have the better. But when you shoot over a pothole or small pond, a dozen blocks usually will suffice.

Never forget that to attract birds your decoys must both look and *act* like live ducks. No matter how fine the blocks, if two or three of them for some reason fail to act the part, the sharp-eyed cagy birds will flare off before they come within gunshot. So leave any faulty decoys home. If some of your blocks sit lopsided on the water, load them so they'll float on an even keel. And keep your rig looking natural as long as you hope for shooting. If anything happens to make one or more decoys look phony, paddle out to remedy the trouble.

Just as important as the naturalness of your decoys is setting them out in the right position in relation to your blind, the direction of the wind, and the flight habits of the ducks you're after.

A flock of dippers may plow in crosswind now and then, but divers rarely do so. They face directly into the wind when they are going to alight on the water, knowing that they must have the assistance of the wind to get into the air again. All ducks are likely to circle your decoys at least once to look things over before they decide to come in. Canvasbacks often cross your decoys high in the air and at top speed; then, while you are cussing because they didn't see your stool, they drop down, circle wide, and come back at much lower speed.

You can't control wind direction or quickly change the location of a permanent blind, but often you can place your set so that when ducks circle they will be likely to fly between you and the decoys.

As for the wind, most duck hunters like it quartering over one shoulder or the other. Many like it blowing from right behind them. Others like it to be blowing at right angles to the face of the blind. *Don't* have it blowing in your face, if you can help it, for then chances are the birds will circle over and behind the blind.

Now for eight suggested layouts. Note that in the illustrations, just to keep things simple, all decoys are heading in the same direction. On occasion, of course, you may want to anchor them in some special way — helter-skelter, perhaps, or mostly facing in.

Sometimes you'll get excellent results with diver ducks by setting out a mixed stool diagonally upwind from your blind, with the closest decoys 15 or 20 yards from it, as in sketch No. 1. We used this rig

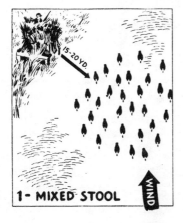

1- MIXED STOOL — 15-20 YD. — WIND

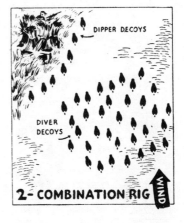

2- COMBINATION RIG — DIPPER DECOYS — DIVER DECOYS — WIND

167

one day when I was shooting redheads from a booby or parlor blind built of brush on pilings 250 yards out from shore on lower Chesapeake Bay. We got our limits.

The next day, shooting from a point blind in about the same position relative to the wind, we added a dozen mallard and black-duck blocks anchored in shallow water close to shore. The combination rig (sketch No. 2) worked fine.

In both cases, when the ducks circled to come to the decoys they flew between the blind and the spread. When ducks do that, even when at the last moment they spot your blocks as fakes you'll get good shots; for as they swerve away from the spread they'll come closer to your blind.

Just a word of warning. Never set diver-duck decoys out in shallow-water. Canvasbacks and other deep-water ducks know they shouldn't be there, and won't come near them.

Now comes perhaps the most important aspect of duck decoying: What particular spread should you use? Naturally, this depends a great deal on the conditions under which you are hunting.

If you have a big expanse of water in front of you, I'd suggest the wide V-spread (sketch No. 3), with stringers running out for 75 yards or more, and some females right in front of you.

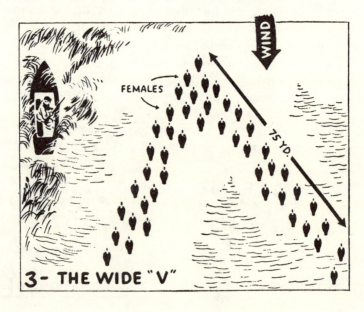

FEMALES

WIND

75 YD.

3- THE WIDE "V"

If there's not so much water in front of you, and therefore only a limited feeding area, the fishhook or J spread (sketch No. 4) should be more effective. It is good for divers in deep water, and for dippers in shallower water. In setting it out for divers, however, remember

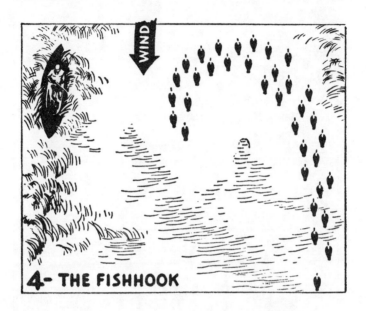

4- THE FISHHOOK

that they usually cross over decoys, so put the long shank of the spread away from you, and the hook right in front of your blind.

Another effective spread for small bodies of water is the triangle or pyramid (sketch No. 5). The smaller the water area the more deadly this spread, since it permits you to mass your stools toward the outside, leaving the center open for birds coming in. Have this unobstructed center opposite your blind, and provide plenty of room for the divers to alight.

There are numerous variations of this spread. You can shape it like a kite or a long, slim arrowhead; or you can bend its upwind side to form an inviting U opening.

An effective layout for deep-water ducks on Chesapeake Bay is shown in sketch No. 6. Most of the decoys — individually anchored — are set fairly close together, in no particular order, but looking natural. Then a dozen or so blocks are anchored trailing away from the main body, at varying intervals which average about five yards.

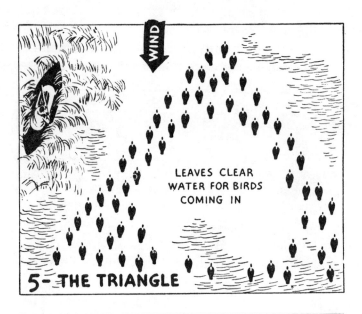

5- THE TRIANGLE

6- LAYOUT WITH STRAGGLERS

This gives the impression of stragglers swimming up to join in the feast that the main bunch has found.

When a large set of decoys is set offshore on a lake or river, it is well to have most of them located slightly downwind from the blind. The entire set should be as close inshore as is practicable, but still far enough out to present a good showing to approaching birds. A very satisfactory method is to place the decoys in a somewhat oval design, with the longer sides paralleling the wind, as in sketch No. 7. The decoys on the upwind side, and on the near and far sides, should be placed closer together than those toward the center and on the downwind side. The spread should cover an area about 25 yards long and 20 yards wide, and should start two or three yards offshore, except

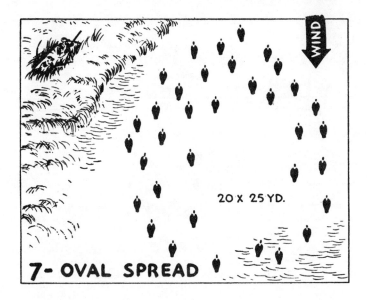

WIND

20 X 25 YD.

7- OVAL SPREAD

perhaps for a few blocks anchored in close along the shoreline. In no place should the decoys be bunched, for that would destroy the effect of loafing and feeding ducks.

Never bunch puddler decoys closely — this makes a picture of uneasy and suspicious birds. When you see swimming ducks gang up, you can be sure that they are frightened and ready to take off. Ducks flying overhead are quick to recognize this fact and lose all interest in that particular locality.

When goose decoys are used, best results will be obtained if they are set in a separate group a little way from the duck blocks. Sketch 8 shows an interesting spread some gunners use for jump-shooting on the upper Susquehanna and Potomac Rivers. At the upwind end are half a dozen goose decoys. Twenty feet downwind from them are a dozen or more canvasback blocks. After another 20-foot break there

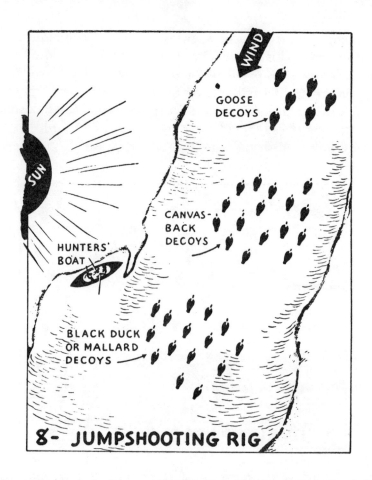

8- JUMPSHOOTING RIG

are as many black-duck or mallard decoys. The hunters conceal them-selves and their paddle boat near shore, and when a flock comes to the rig they try to get close enough for shots as the alarmed birds rise. One of the tricks of the trade is to set the decoys so that the sun will be back of the boat, and in the ducks' eyes, as the hunters make their approach.

The way things are today, it costs most of us hunters plenty in time and money just to get into a good duck-shooting area. We might profitably spend a little more of both on study and preparation, and so get more sport — and ducks.

CHAPTER XX

Training the Hunting Dog

The right start in teaching a pup the
fundamentals will pay off for
years in the field

BY McDOWELL LYON

O F ALL the questions dog owners ask, the one put most frequently
is, "At what age should I start training my pup?" The answer
usually given is, "As early in the pup's life as possible," which means
about the fourth or fifth month, but that needs a little explaining.
Actually, a more specific answer depends largely on what the owner
has in mind when he speaks of training. There's basic training and
advanced training, and the proper time when each should be under-
taken necessarily must be determined by the dog's ability to respond
— his intellectual capacity, in other words.

Some idea of what to aim for in figuring out training schedules
for pups can be found in the accepted field-trial rules and practices.
In what is known as the Puppy Stakes, which is for dogs under 1 year
old, no birds are liberated on the course, and no bird work is expected
of the entrants. In fact, it's rare for birds to be liberated in the Derby
Stakes, which include dogs that are under 2 years old. Dogs in that
category are judged pretty much on the same basis as those in the
Puppy Stakes so far as range and ground coverage are concerned, and
no consideration is given to actual bird work. The tip-off in this is that
ordinarily advanced training isn't started until a dog is at least 1 year
old. But basic training is something else again.

I've often felt that many amateurs who take on the training of their dogs frequently expect, and sometimes demand, far too much entirely too soon. They force advanced training on dogs that haven't had enough basic training, and that are too immature mentally to cope with involved problems. What, then, can one use as a guide to a dog's capacity for education?

You won't go far wrong in figuring the timing of your dog's mental development and capacity to absorb instruction if you compare it with that of a human being approximately in the ratio of one month to one year. When a pup is between 6 and 12 months old, educationally he should be going through kindergarten and grammar school. After that he's ready for high school and later, perhaps, for college. From this rough yardstick, it's easy to see how unreasonable it is to expect a pup a year old or less to learn the equivalent of mathematics and chemistry. He'll be doing all right if he's mastered his three R's by that time.

Basic training for dogs can be likened to kindergarten for children. It cultivates the normal aptitudes and prepares the mind and the emotions for bigger things to come.

The first lessons are simple but important since they lay the foundation for mature training. During this period the dog should be taught a negative command, to heel on a lead, sit, and the beginnings of his recall and stop-on-command orders. This early instruction may be given in many different ways, but I'll outline the methods I've found work best.

Do everything you can as early as possible to familiarize the pup with his name. When he learns to respond to it, combine the name with a command. This serves two purposes; it attracts the pup's attention and makes him alert to expect and obey an action command. The association of the two will help to avoid confusion later when the pup works afield with other dogs that are being given commands by owners or handlers.

The two main commands to get started at this time are the positive and negative. It's been my experience that dogs react more quickly and more readily to the sibilant, or hissing, sounds than to most others. Words with s, sh, z, and zh in them are good to use in giving positive commands. They encourage the dog to do what you want him to do, and to keep on doing it until you stop him. Dogs will respond to the work "sick" the first time they hear it. You'll find similar sounds, spoken as commands, useful in getting your dogs to range or work out from you.

The standard command for stopping a dog in action is "whoa," but I've found the harsher "ack" or "hah" more effective in giving negative orders. Likewise, "nix" or "nah" produce quicker compliance than just plain "no."

Some trainers prefer to use whistles in giving commands — one sharp blast as a negative, a rolling note to keep on going, and two sharp notes as a recall. I've no objection to whistles, but it seems to me that the majority of whistlers never seem to know when to stop. And any sound that is repeated too often, whether a whistle or a word, invariably produces such a state of confusion in a dog that effective compliance is impossible.

You can start teaching your dog these simple affirmative and negative commands around the feed pan. Teach the negative command first.

To show the dog what you want him to do when he hears this sound, place his feed pan on the floor and, as he rushes to it, give the command "ach" and restrain him by holding your hand, palm toward him, in front of his nose. Hold him off, even if he circles or jumps around, and repeat the word several times. Then release him with an "O.K." Give this lesson as often as necessary, holding the pup off from the feed pan for progressively longer intervals until he gets the idea.

When he thoroughly understands what "ach" means, use it in conjunction with "whoa" so that both commands become associated with cease motion, stay put, or positive restraint on any contemplated action. The command word meaning sit also may be introduced later and become a part of this exercise in restraint. Keep plugging at the negative command whenever the opportunity arises. Use it occasionally even on minor things just to broaden its influence.

It is important never to give a command unless you're in a position to enforce obedience to it. Obedience must be insisted upon until the time comes when the dog complies with the command automatically. If you force obedience twice but not the third time, the likelihood is you'll set up doubts in your dog's mind about just how far he must go in respecting your orders.

175

For the same reason, avoid using any command that the dog previously has learned to disobey. The command "come here" is a good example. Those words often are used when a pup is romping about the house or yard. You speak them, repeat them, shout them, but the pup ignores you and continues on his merry way. He's so cute you let him get away with it. Soon the command means nothing to him; he can disobey it and nothing unpleasant happens to him. If this applies in your case, don't use "come here" when you start seriously to train your dog. Use a different command, or give the old command a new twist — something like "hi here."

Much of this early, basic training should center around preventing bad habits from becoming established. There are many things that seem harmless and funny when a pup does them that can become mighty disagreeable when projected into misbehavior later in life. It's laughable to see a tiny pup grab a trouser leg and shake it, chase birds out of the yard, or get himself all wrapped up in an old towel he starts to tussle with. But if these funny tricks are encouraged they easily can develop into not-so-funny tricks like nipping the legs of guests, chasing automobiles, and romping off with your freshly laundered shirt. It's best to put a quick end to these potentially bad habits. Train your pup to behave, and train him to obey just as soon as you can.

In correcting his indiscretions, try to remember not to expect more of the pup than he's capable of giving. Don't give him a chance to make that first mistake. That's not easy, I know, but it will pay off in the long run. Just as in humans, a bad habit once formed by a dog is difficult to break.

Don't give the pup free run of the entire house unless you can watch him all the time. Keep him in a small area of the kitchen or some other room. Cover this area with papers and eventually reduce the spread of them to a small section of the improvised pen. Housebreaking scents will speed the training. Feed and exercise the pup regularly over the ground outdoors that you want him to use for these purposes. This care, plus a little maturity, will make a gentleman out of your pup much quicker than shouting or nose rubbing.

Today, fortunately, clubs that conduct obedience courses in dog training are located within reach of most dog owners. In many cases provision is made for the owner himself to put his dog through the classes under the supervision of a skilled trainer. It's a job worth undertaking. If there are no such clubs within comfortable traveling distance of your home, I strongly suggest that you consult any one of several good, inexpensive books on the subject.

After he's 7 months old, give your dog as much of this basic obedience training as you have time for, but don't make the exercises so long that they tire the dog. Take it easy. At first your dog may appear depressed when you start ordering him about, especially if you're positive with him. That's natural. After all, up to then you've let him gallop freely, come and go as he liked. Now you're dictating to him. His reaction very likely will be similar to that of your young son when you call him in from the ball game across the street. But the pup will soon get over it.

A collar and lead come next in the training program. There are several procedures you might try in getting your pup acquainted with them. One is to put a collar on him and have a 2 to 6-in. cord hanging from it. As he romps and plays with the cord, take hold of it and pull him around a bit. He'll think you're playing with him, but in time he will learn to respond to the tugging of the lead. Another is to anchor him to a pipe, fence, or stanchion with a light chain lead. This will teach him what the lead is for without having him associate the disagreeable aspects of restraint with you.

A third procedure is to put a lead on him, take off on a slow walk, and have him follow you — skidding or otherwise. His desire for comfort will soon bring him in line. This usually is the quickest method, but it may not be the best one if the pup is inclined to be shy or soft. No matter which way you handle it, you can expect bronco antics during the first few lead-training lessons.

Now we come to heeling. Pointers and setters often are broken to walk on the right side of a gunner, but heeling on the left side is compulsory in obedience, spaniel, and retriever trials. For this reason most owners train their pups to heel on the left with the shoulder on line with the walker's leg.

Walk the dog around the yard in this position. Use a light switch to tap him when he gets out of place. Or a sharp jerk, never a pull, on his collar usually will snap him back into line. Repeat the command "heel" at various intervals, every time you correct him, and when you change directions so that the word becomes associated with the position.

When he begins to heel reasonably well, start training him to sit when you stop. To vary this command from the conversational "sit" give it the sound "z" — something like "zit-z-z." Hold the lead in your right hand, directly above the pup's head and taut enough to keep him from settling in front. Repeat the command "zit-z-z" and force him down in the sitting position. Do this by squeezing his loin muscles and pressing downward with your left hand. He'll probably give way under the pressure of the squeeze, but you may have to be emphatic a time or two. If he starts to get up as soon as you remove your hands, repeat the command and the pressure.

When the pup has learned to sit at heel, train him to sit when you're in front of him and facing him. To do this, stand in front of him and give the command "zit-z-z." As you do so, swing your right hand upward and grasp the pup's lower jaw, hold him up in front, and press downward on his loins. The upward movement of your right hand should be emphatic so that eventually the motion will become a signal in itself.

The next move is to hold the palm of your hand in front of the dog's nose and command him to stay. This command can be "stay," "steady," or "whoa." If he starts to break away, repeat the command and force him into position. The negative "ach" also will help to prevent him from breaking, particularly if it has been hooked in with the "whoa" at the feed pan.

Now back away the length of a 3-ft. lead. Make the pup hold the sitting position for a few seconds, then command him to come to you. The command word I use for this is "hi-here." When a whistle is to be used in the field it can be connected with this as the training progresses. One long blast is to come in and two short blasts are to go out.

As you give the pup the command to come to you, reel him in promptly and emphatically. Then make him sit again in front of you. Enforce instantaneous response from the very beginning and maintain it until the dog complies automatically. The future response you will have in getting the dog to come to you on command depends on how well he learns this foundation exercise.

When the dog has learned to respond to command on the 3-ft. lead, attach him to a 25-ft. line and gradually increase the distances you back away from him. At this stage of the training you can start walking to the left and right of the dog, or completely around him. This will make him steady regardless of your position.

These simple exercises should carry the dog beyond his seventh month. If they are firmly established, you'll be surprised how easy it will be to take him into advanced training. As you work with your pup keep these four things in mind: 1. Never give a command that you can't enforce until the dog is thoroughly responsive to it. 2. Don't nag or pick at the dog; give the command and enforce immediate response. 3. Don't make the exercises too long so that the pup gets tired. 4. Don't expect more of him than he's capable of giving.

One more thing. Overly petting and complimenting a pup during training often does more harm than good. It gets his mind off his business. Eliminate repeated pats and "good doggy" talk. A firm pressure of your hand and a slight kneading of the pup's skin will be more effective and it won't set him off into nonrelated acrobatics.

The amount of time that may be required in giving this primary instruction depends on your application and how well you avoid confusing the dog. Give him a chance to play and romp, but make him conscious of the fact that training is school and that he has a job to do.

It's my personal opinion that no puppy is ever really trained — at least in the true sense of that word. He may be developed, educated, or otherwise prepared for training. But it takes time — maturity — to bring a dog to a point where he's ready for real, purposeful training. Until that maturity is reached, be content to let your dog master the elementary subjects on the curriculum. If you do you'll save yourself the embarrassment, time, and expense of having to do what some sportsmen I know find necessary — having their dogs retrained every bird season. The mistake those men made was in rushing their dogs. They tried to make bird dogs out of mischievous, fun-loving pups. It can't be done.

Some of the training clubs offer courses in advanced obedience work. This covers such exercises as retrieving, directional field work, and trailing. Such instruction provides a good foundation on which to build a fine field dog.

Just when is the best time to start actual game work depends on what kind of dog you have and what game you're interested in. If you hunt for quail or chukars in open territory, you'll want your dog to get out and keep on going until he hits bird scent. What he does after that depends largely on the basic training he's had. But I'm strongly against putting field restraints on a dog until he's at least 15 months old. You can do all the yard training you want, but when you first take your dog in the field, let him go. Don't hold him.

Of course, some hunters don't want the big-going dog, and while all flush dogs should be enthusiastic, they shouldn't be wide workers since they must remain within gunshot range. If the "whoa" or negative command has been firmly taught, any dog can be held down to any desired pace. If your dog's had the primary negative and affirmative commands sufficiently drilled into him so that responding to them has become second nature, then you'll have no trouble holding him to the pace you want, no birds flushed out of gun range, nor any other undesirable performances that might occur afield.

And don't think it sissified to train your dog to be a good home companion. To become properly housebroken should be one of the first achievements of any good sporting dog. With the exception of hounds maintained in certain sections of the country, most dogs are kept outdoors exclusively only during the limited hunting season. The rest of the time they're at home with their owners, and it's a wanton loss of their companionship to relegate them to life in a cabin or box. It's surprising how many owners ask whether housebreaking lessens a dog's hunting ability. The answer is an emphatic "no."

Frank of Sunnylawn, a pointer that broke the world record for amateur wins, was as much a part of Charlie Farrer's home as he was proficient in the field. Mississippi Zev, winner of both the professional and amateur national quail championship stakes, was 80 percent house pet and 20 percent field dog. His owner was proud to have him win two national stakes, but he was even prouder to have him as part of the family.

Two of the greatest hounds I've ever seen work on wolves and big cats shared the beds with their owner. And I must say that I was flattered when Red Joe once left his owner's bed and crawled in with me. He was a softie? Not so's you'd notice it. He held a grizzly at bay single-handedly for five hours until the rest of the pack and the hunters came up to relieve him.

So don't worry about making a pet of your hunting dog. If he's got the right breeding and you give him the proper training, he'll be able to lick the syrup off your pancake plate in the morning, point quail for you in the afternoon, and then maybe tree a coon by moonlight.

Often dogs turned out by professional trainers are top grade because they respond with mechanical perfection. That usually can't be said of dogs owned and trained by amateurs. But the amateur owner and trainer can get much more out of his dog than any professional can. He can get companionship and personal understanding if he'll only give the dog a chance to live with him and learn to love him.

CHAPTER XXI

Hunting on Horseback

What every hunter who rides should know about equipment and his mount

BY JACK O'CONNOR

E VERY fall sees hundreds if not thousands of earnest hunters perched for the first time on the quarter-decks of an equal number of not-so-fiery steeds so a-hunting they can go. From Mexico to the Yukon, they jog painfully along trails, crawl slowly up mountains, hunting everything from Mexican white-tail deer to Dall sheep. The strange creatures on which they sit have no clutch and no brake. Their steering mechanism, these horsemen learn, is very imperfect, as those who have had their shins raked by bark and their legs punctured by sharp snags can testify.

But still these plugs have their advantages. They can go places where a jeep couldn't get to first base. They provide wind and muscle for those who do not have them. Often a horse will even supply eyes for the hunter and spot game before his rider will. Mountain horses seem even to be equipped with self-setting gyrocompasses which will take the lost hunter back to his tent. Further, horses can see in the dark; more than once they have taken me to camp at times when I couldn't have seen my hand in a white glove before my face.

The horse is one of the most gifted and one of the dumbest animals in the world. The same horse that will unerringly retrace his steps to camp on the blackest night may be put into screaming panic by a chewing-gum wrapper or a blowing cigarette paper.

Ranchers and outfitters know that most city hunters are neither cowboys nor jockeys, and they usually put them on staid, calm plugs that have long since sown their wild oats, yet the oldest and calmest horse can still go into a wild and unreasoning panic.

With the scabbard at the left rear, O'Connor can dismount and get at his rifle, all in one quick motion.

The man who hunts on horseback should never forget that his horse is not a machine, that it is magnificently gifted with muscles and instincts; but that it is a relatively brainless animal that can crush a rider with its weight, kick him to death in a panic, or drag him until he is a bloody pulp if his foot should get hung up in a stirrup.

The first thing the guide does when he puts a pilgrim aboard a cayuse is to ask him if the stirrups are all right. Most of the time that is about on a par with a doctor's asking a child if he ought to take some aspirin, go on a buttermilk diet, or have his tonsils removed. The tot doesn't know and neither does the dude.

Many practicing cowboys ride a rather short stirrup so that if a running horse falls with them, they will be thrown clear. Stirrups so adjusted, however, will beat the average dude hunter to death. His calves and the inside of his legs will be so sore that at the end of the first day he will not want to ride again for a week. On the other hand, a too-long stirrup causes all the wear and tear to be taken by the portion of the anatomy that comes in contact with the saddle.

For most men the stirrups are correctly adjusted when the rider's seat clears his saddle by from four to six inches when he stands up in the stirrups. Remember this, get your stirrups so adjusted, and the hunt on horseback will be much easier.

Once the stirrups are properly adjusted, the next problem is putting on a rifle scabbard. If our horseback hunter has a good one he is a very lucky fellow. Most saddle scabbards are too small, too short, too skimpy. In fact, the only good ones I have seen have been made to order. If there is, in these United States, a first-rate store-bought saddle scabbard for a scope-sighted rifle with a 24-inch barrel like the Model 70 Winchester I have yet to come across it. The ones most often seen do not cover enough of the buttstock. They do not protect it from scratches of brush and twigs and they will not keep rain, snow, and sleet from obscuring the objective lens of the scope.

Years ago a friend and I worked out the dimensions of a saddle scabbard which has since been duplicated many times and which has seen service from Alaska to Mexico. For a scope-sighted bolt-action rifle with a 24-inch barrel, the scabbard should be 39½ inches long, 9½ inches wide at the top, and 6 inches wide in the middle. The straps by which it is tied to the saddle should be 52 inches long. The scabbard should be made of good saddle-skirting leather so that it will protect the rifle and scope and also so that the rifle will not jounce around and wear off the bluing. A scabbard of this sort can also be used as a carrying case by having buckles on the sides so a boot can be strapped on to protect the butt.

The problem of just how to put the scabbard on the saddle remains.

If the back of the horse is properly shaped to retain a saddle and if the horse is actually to be used to hunt from, as is often the case in the West, the scabbard should be on the left side with the butt to the rear. The scabbard, pointing muzzle-down, should hang at an angle of about 45 degrees, and then the rifle will not be lost even when going up a steep hill. The scabbard should be inside the stirrup

Four good saddle rifles (top to bottom): Very accurate 7mm. with Weaver K-4 scope. Next, Mannlicher-Schoenauer .270 with "butter-knife" bolt handle is thin and handy. The Marlin's Model 336 carbine in .35 Remington—fast and effective if range is not too long. At bottom, the classic .30/30 saddle carbine, a Winchester Model 94.

leather; otherwise it has a tendency to twist the stirrup and cause a cramp in the left leg.

This position for carrying the rifle shines in the hunting field. In many sections of the West, the country is easy enough so that the hunter can ride around the heads of canyons and move deer. He then gets off his horse on the left side, reaches back for the butt of his rifle, and yanks it out. Even if the horse is frightened and bolts, he still has his hand on the rifle and will get his shot. He can look up his horse later.

With the butt to the rear, the rifle cannot catch on a limb and tear the scabbard off, nor does the scabbard fill up with leaves, twigs, and debris in general.

The worst place I can think of for carrying a rifle is butt forward on the left side parallel to the horse's neck. In this position the scabbard fills up with twigs, and the rifle is liable to snag on a limb and get torn off. Even worse, perhaps, is that the hunter has to drag his rifle butt past the head of the horse. The horse senses the excitement when the hunter jumps a buck and scrambles to the ground. Then when he makes a grab for something near its head the horse is often so frightened that it will bolt — and take the rifle with it. Even if it runs only twenty yards and stops, it will usually ruin the hunter's chances for a shot.

In much of western Canada the horses have a high proportion of Percheron and other cold-blooded breeds in their make-up, and their backs simply are not shaped to take saddles properly. If the weight is not well distributed, the saddles will pull over. In the northern Rockies, though, the hunter rarely jumps off, grabs his rifle, and shoots. Instead he uses his horse on the trail or to go to the foot of the mountain where he is to make his climb.

In this case the place to carry a rifle is where it has less tendency to pull the saddle over. On a nag such as those we have described, carrying the butt to the rear causes the saddle to pull over toward the side the rifle is on, as the cinch is far forward just behind the horse's forelegs. Carrying the rifle on the left side is particularly bad, because the hunter gets on and off on that side and his weight on the stirrup, plus that of the rifle, tends to pull the saddle over.

In what I'll call the *trail* position, then, the rifle is carried on the right side, butt forward with the muzzle sharply down. This way the weight is squarely on the cinch and the rifle does not have enough leverage to twist the saddle, as it would if the butt were to the rear. It is a very clumsy location if the hunter has to pile off, grab his rifle, and take a quick shot; but it enables the saddle to ride on an even keel — and that's what's needed in this case. The weight of the rifle has a slight tendency to pull the saddle to the right, but every time the hunter gets on or off, his weight on the left stirrup pulls the saddle a bit to the left and corrects it.

Other positions are used and described, but I cannot see them — particularly for a fairly heavy, bolt-action rifle.

Most hunters carry too much junk with them on their horses. They get saddlebags and fill them full. There is no use loading down a

186

horse with useless equipment that will not be needed on the trip.

The average hunter stays on his horse too much. He sits there like a sack of potatoes being carried to market and rides slowly along the side of a canyon waiting for a buck to jump out on the other side. In certain areas where deer are plentiful and there's not too much cover, this passive method is frequently successful, but in most places it

The trail position—when you're merely going to where you'll start your hunt on foot, and won't use your rifle meantime—has the virtue of not pulling the saddle over on a round-backed horse. Note that the rifle is on the horse's right side.

leaves too much to the co-operation and good will of the deer. It is the method used by cowboys who are not hunters but who are called on to guide now and then. In the course of their work they see deer. They remember where they see them. Most of them don't like to walk anyway, so if they guide they simply ride around where they have seen deer and hope for the best.

In deer hunting the hunter should use his horse only to get into likely country. The actual *hunting* should be done on foot. During most of the hunting day deer are lying down, dozing, thinking matters over. Only the dumb ones come barging out when a cavalcade comes stumbling along the mountainside. The smart ones lie doggo.

But suppose our hunters tie their horses and begin to work out the heads of the canyons and the brush under the rimrocks. The bucks get nervous. The longer the hunters hang around, the more jittery they get. Presently one of them decides to make a sneak for it, and the battle begins. *In both horseback and foot hunting, then, it isn't how much country you cover but how well you cover it.*

Many parts of the West are open and so easy to get around in that a man on a horse can do a pretty fair job of hunting it, and except for the fact that it takes him longer to get into action, he is not handicapped. In rugged, rocky, and brushy country, though, he does better off the horse than on.

The old saying that a horse can go anywhere a man can go is dangerously untrue. A horse can go over some surprising country, but a man can go where a horse would break his neck.

I have seen places where a horse could take a man right up among the sheep and goats, but they are exceptions. They include parts of the Canadian Rockies, where the typical mountain is a long, fairly gentle incline on one side and almost a straight up-and-down bluff on the other. It is no trick to ride up the gentle slope, then get off and hunt the points and ledges on foot.

In most sheep and goat country, however, the horse is a nuisance. Even taking a horse out from camp and tying it close to the mountain is a sour idea, because half the time the poor weary hunter will have to make a long and painful journey back to get his horse.

Most sheep country is so rough that it absolutely cannot be negotiated by a horse — or by any other large mammal except a sheep or a properly shod human being with muscles in his legs. I say *most*, but not all, by any means. Sheep country that can be hunted from horseback usually does not remain sheep country long.

One rule the horseback hunter should never forget is to get off his horse and lead when the footing gets bad — and that means any place where a slip or a stumble would mean a bad fall. A panic-stricken, struggling horse, 1,200 pounds of bone and muscle, is bad business to get mixed up with. Not a few citizens are killed or crippled every year because they were in the saddle at a time when they should have been out of it — and that includes crack riders.

The fact that more horseback hunters don't meet their doom annually fills me with mild and innocent wonder, for many of these characters know so little about a horse that they have no notion as to where he can go safely and where he cannot.

The horse is a great invention for getting the hunter into the hunting country, but he is even more useful in getting the game back to camp. A good, stout horse can wobble into camp with the head and two quarters of a moose, and for one to carry in a buck is routine.

A big buck is hard to pack, however, and continually slides over on the side the head is on. Here is a packing method that works. Drape

On a round-backed horse this position has less tendency to pull the saddle awry but has little else to recommend it. In ducking a limb, you may knock your teeth against the butt.

the buck across the saddle with the belly toward the horn and the weight equally distributed. Then cut a hole in the belly skin and hook it over the horn. Next pull the head *back* and tie it firmly with the saddle strings near the cantle. Break the legs at the knee so they will not catch on limbs and brush. Then cut slits in all four legs just above the knee, pass a rope through one pair of slits and tie it, bring the free end under the horse — preferably so that it rides on the cinch and will not gall him — and secure it to the other pair of slits.

If the hunter wishes, has the rope, and knows how, he can throw a hitch on the buck, but the method I have described will get him back to camp. By buttoning the hole in the belly flap over the saddle horn and holding the head and flanks in place with the saddle strings, I have taken bucks into camp with no rope whatsoever.

Anyone who plans to use a horse in his hunting as a regular thing should put some thought into choosing a rifle for the purpose.

There are really three sorts of people who carry rifles around on a horse: the working horseman, the mounted hunter, and the man who rides into hunting country and then hunts afoot. The working horseman — the rancher, the mounted law-enforcement officer, etc. —

No rope along? Just button a hole cut in the deer's belly skin to the saddle horn, tie head and flanks with saddle strings. This time the scabbard rode best as shown.

must ride constantly and often at a gallop. He wants an effective rifle that does not interfere with his riding, does not bounce around when the horse gets out of a walk, and does not cramp his leg. He also wants one he can jerk out of the scabbard instantly. Such a weapon should be short, light, flat. Ideally it should also use a cartridge giving flat trajectory and good accuracy. Because the horse is a noisy beast, very often game or a varmint must be shot at on the run and at considerable range.

The man who merely hunts on horseback and does not carry a rifle as part of daily routine can stand a somewhat longer and heavier

190

weapon. But even he wants a fairly light, short rifle. In many parts of the West and Southwest the country is open and smooth, and the hunter can ride along the sides of canyons and around the heads of draws, shooting deer that jump out.

In many areas, though where country is too rough or too brushy to be hunted from horseback, the sportsman merely rides out to the gen-

If you expect to spot your buck while on horseback, jump off, grab your rifle and shoot, here's how to have the scabbard. That strapped-in boot protects the rifle butt from scratches.

eral area where he plans to hunt and then makes his climb or stalk on foot. Then any adequate rifle will do; it does not have to be a saddle model at all. It can weigh 12 lb. and have a barrel 26 in. long— as witness some of the weird weapons hunters take with them into the Rocky Mountains.

The all-time favorite among short saddle rifles is the Winchester Model 94 carbine. With its 20-in. barrel it is short, light, flat, and handy. It is also rugged and dependable and is the wilderness favorite from Mexico to the Arctic. The Model 94, besides being relatively cheap, is light and rugged — a natural for the cattleman who wants to polish off an occasional coyote, shoot a mountain lion his dog puts up a tree, or collect a buck for the table without too much bother.

The horseback hunter's rifle, as opposed to the rifle carried as a tool by the working horseman, should be a sort of lightweight jack-of-all-trades — accurate and flat-shooting enough to knock off a coyote at 300 yd., light enough to carry around in a steep and rugged canyon if the hunter has to take off on foot, rugged enough to withstand a lot of jouncing around in a saddle scabbard, short enough to be handy.

Because most country where horseback hunting is practical is fairly open, the cartridge for the big-game hunter's saddle rifle should drive its bullet at about 3,000 foot seconds' muzzle velocity, not only for flat trajectory and minimum lead on running game but for knock-down power with the occasional poorly placed shot. I've used a good many different calibers for horseback hunting, ranging all the way from the .250/3000 Savage to the .35 Whelen, but the stand-outs among factory cartridges are the .270 with the 130-gr. bullet, the .30/06 with the 150-gr. bullet, and the 7x57 mm. Mauser with the 130 or 140-gr. bullet. All have good range and plenty of knockdown power, particularly on deer-size animals. Some of the larger wildcats, such as the .25, .270, and 7 mm. Magnums of the Weatherby and Ackley series, are, if kept light, excellent for saddle use. In the hands of a good shot and on deer-size animals even the little .250/3000 and the .257 do very well.

The rifle itself should weigh around 7-7½ lb. with iron sights, ideally no more than 8 with scope and mount. Barrel should be from 20 to 22 in. long.

With the proper equipment and a healthy respect for the peculiarities of his mount, the hunter on horseback can increase his sport and his skill.

CHAPTER XXII

Dressing and Curing Game

**Proper handling of your kill from the
time it is shot until you get the meat
home will insure good eating and
valuable hides**

BY MAURICE H. DECKER

E VERY year a vast quantity of big-game meat is eaten and enjoyed.
And every year another vast quantity is thrown away as unfit to
eat. That's unfortunate, for originally most game meat is clean, sweet,
and flavorsome, and becomes rank only because it is˙badly handled.
And the critical handling time comes in the first few hours after the
animal is killed.

Heat is the villain in the piece—heat and certain glands. The
glands must be removed promptly, the abdominal cavity cleaned,
and the body cooled. Sometimes still another factor enters into the
case — a long chase of a wounded animal. The attempt to escape
produces a feverish condition in the animal and that tends to impart
a strong flavor to the meat.

Cooling means letting the body heat escape from the carcass. The
sooner this starts, and the faster it proceeds, the better your game will
taste. Inadequate cooling is probably the biggest reason why venison
and elk meat sometimes taste bad. And the danger of insufficient
cooling is very great in mild weather. Then improperly cooled game
may sour after it is placed in a quick freeze or freezer locker.

In cold weather you can work leisurely in dressing out big game.

You don't have to hang the carcass right away, and you can leave its hide on to protect the meat during the journey home. But when days are warm and humid — humidity is especially detrimental — work fast! Do everything you can to speed up cooling.

Empty the abdominal cavity immediately; this operation alone removes a big source of heat and fermentation. Get the carcass off the ground so that air can circulate completely around it. Separate it into quarters as soon as it's convenient and legal to do so. (The legal caution applies only in states that require identification of sex before dismemberment.)

Before you start to dress out a big-game animal be sure it is stone dead, not merely unconscious. Shoot again if there's any doubt, because a buck deer or bull elk that suddenly comes alive from the prick of your skinning knife can be an ugly customer. Some hunters insist upon sticking game to expedite bleeding. A gash across the throat accomplishes this best but is likely to spoil the head for mounting. The alternative is to shove the knife deep into the breast at the base of the neck, then twist its point sideways to sever the big arteries. Sometimes a well-expanded bullet does a fair job of bleeding.

Before sticking, pull the head backward toward the shoulders so it won't become bloodstained. If the animal lies on sloping ground, twist it around so the belly is downhill, because a lot of blood and paunch excreta will emerge during your work and its easier to keep the meat clean if you let the refuse run away by gravity. Sometimes you can hasten bleeding by working the legs back and forth vigorously to empty the large veins. Again, be sure the beast is stone dead before you grab its foot.

You need a large abdominal opening to empty the paunch, so cut down the middle of the belly from the breastbone to the anus. But before you do this, take steps to protect the meat from musky gland odors and taint from excretions of anus and genitals. Deer have scent glands near the hock of each hind leg. They're marked by tufts of hair. Slice these glands away, cutting down to the bone to be sure of removing all objectionable material. Take care not to touch the glands, or your hands will carry their taint to the meat.

Also cut around the anus and genitals so they and surrounding hair and skin can be laid back away from the carcass and tied securely with string. Be sure urine doesn't touch meat for in some species it gives a very disagreeable flavor that penetrates deeply from surface contact. When you've done these things wash your hands in cold water or snow, or wipe them well on cloth, leaves, or grass before you proceed further.

When opening the belly, insert two fingers of the left hand under the skin and spread them a little to make room for the knife. As you proceed, press intestines and stomach back so you won't cut into them. The fingers also guide the blade. Let the entrails roll out, freeing them with the knife where necessary. Remove and save heart and liver. Cut away lungs, reaching up into the neck as far as possible to sever gullet and windpipe. Dressing and quartering are much easier if you have a light ax to chop through rib cage and down between the hams.

In wooded country it isn't hard to hang a deer; one man can do it if he carries a short piece of rope, as most hunters do, and he won't strain his back either if he uses a woodsman's stunt to concentrate his strength. One way is to bend a springy sapling down with your weight and tie its top to the deer. When you release your hold its resilience helps raise the dead weight. Or procure three poles, tie them into a tripod, and spread butts wide so the tops are near the ground. Hitch your deer to their juncture and lift by pushing the poles inward, one at a time, thus raising the center. A rather heavy carcass can be elevated by this plan if you go slowly.

To cool or dress a deer, you can hang it by the head or by the heels. Either way expedites escape of body heat, but head hanging is better if you plan to save the head horns and don't want them bloodstained. The lifting rope can be tied to the horns. To heel-hang a carcass, cut a gambrel stick, sharpen its ends, and push it through cuts made in the hock skin between the big tendon and the bone. When you are able to lift only part of a heavy carcass, elevate the rear quarters because they have thicker meat and need more time to cool than the shoulders.

You have to figure out something different when game is killed in treeless regions. If there is brush, cut a pile and lay the carcass on top. Build the heap high enough so that when it compresses, the meat is still a couple of feet off the ground. Sometimes you can lay a deer or antelope across a couple of tent poles or rocks so air circulates underneath. Always prop the body cavity open with a spreader stick so air flows inside; do this too when game is hung from trees.

When the rough dressing out is finished, a little fancy work is in order on blood clots, rough edges, and bloodshot tissues about the bullet hole. Cut the bad spots away and smooth up edges to eliminate pockets where moisture, flies, or bacteria could lodge. Wipe out the inside of the cavity if you have material available. Some hunters carry clean cloth for this, others use grass or leaves. It is best not to wash the cavity with water; bloody areas can be scraped clean with your knife.

Blow flies, if they're in season, will promptly get in their licks and lay maggot-hatching eggs in raw surfaces. Cloth bags to enclose the carcass or the quarters are the best protection against them, but you should use the bags judiciously and be sure the fabric is not thick enough to retard cooling. Bags usually measure about 3 x 3½ or 3 x 4 ft.; yardage carried to drape over the belly of an intact carcass can be 12 to 15 ft. long. If small areas of meat are still exposed, rub blood from around the heart over them. It dries into a hard layer that flies won't sting through. Or sprinkle exposed meat liberally with black pepper to repel their attacks.

Since a skinned, quartered carcass cools more than twice as quickly as a whole one, perform these operations as soon as possible when game is taken in warm weather. When temperatures are cold it is best to leave small and medium-size animals whole, because they cool anyway and the hide protects the meat in transit. Large game like moose must be quartered before it can be handled. Quartering can follow rough dressing and the spread-down hide will protect the meat from dirt until you get it into your cloth bags.

Hung game should be protected from rain, snow, and sun. All wreak havoc with the meat's keeping qualities. In bad weather it may be necessary to erect a tarp above the meat rack or pole. When big game is shot in rough terrain you may have to leave the dressed, cooling carcass on the ground or in a tree overnight until you can get help to bring it in. Then a hanging carcass should be protected from jays and magpies with cloth bags. If you must leave it on the ground, cover it lightly with brush. Your man scent will usually keep small predatory animals away; to be doubly sure, tie some personal article like a handkerchief to the meat.

Cooling should be completely finished before game is transported any great distance. Much meat sours when impatient hunters throw half-cooled carcasses across auto fenders and start home. In warm weather it is safer to spend another day in camp so the meat can hang that much longer. Then in early morning, when it is still cool from the night's chill, wrap it in a blanket or quilt to keep out sun heat and begin the return trip.

If you stop overnight en route, unpack the meat so air can again reach it, suspending it from a tree or laying it atop the car. Repack it before sunrise. Carrying game on a fender close to the hot engine is risky unless the weather is quite cold. The trunk is a cooler place, especially if you can fix its cover partly open or if you have special ventilators installed in its sides. A luggage rack atop the car is also better than the fenders.

Game may be preserved at the camp before transportation by any one of three methods: refrigeration, salting, or dry-curing. When facilities for the first two are unavailable, as often is the case in wilderness camps and on very long trails, hunters must rely upon the third. Dry-curing requires more work and attention, but the finished product is quite tasty and will keep for a long time.

Originally the term "jerked" applied to meat cured without salt. Now it has been extended to cover both salted and unsalted cures. "Jerky" is made easiest in the thin, dry air of the Western plains and deserts, where it is often cured by the sun and wind alone. In other climates artificial heat is necessary to preserve the meat before it starts to spoil.

Dry only the lean, red meat of a game animal, because fatty tissue is likely to turn rancid with age; if possible, use only the tenderest cuts. If the game has just been killed, hang the chosen sections in a shaded spot until all body heat is gone, then slice in pieces ½ in. thick, 5 to 6 in. long, and 2 or 3 in. wide.

It is advisable to use a small wood fire even when you cure meat in arid regions, because it speeds up the process and also drives blowflies away. Drying should continue until the pieces are as hard and brittle as chips. This may require as long as 3 weeks for sun drying, 3 or 4 days when a fire is employed, because lean meat may contain up to 60 percent moisture.

When you use artificial heat, a fire and a drying rack built of stakes and poles are all the equipment needed. Make the rack by driving four stakes with "Y" tops at the corners of a 4-ft. square so they stand about 3½ ft. above the ground. Lay two cross poles in the forks and cover them with slender sticks set about 3 in. apart, on which the pieces of meat are tied, wired, or impaled. With a rack of this size you can use a small, easily controlled fire. Erect a windbreak on one or two sides of the fire under the rack, if necessary, to confine the heat below the meat.

Keep the fire low so it will exhaust moisture from the meat without cooking it, and use fuel that gives a minimum of smoke. Birch is one of the best woods, pine one of the poorest. In most cases the hunter must employ whatever kind he has plenty of, but you should avoid resinous wood if possible.

Shift the meat-supporting poles about on the rack every hour or two so that all receive even exposure. If drying isn't completed at nightfall, let the fire go out and cover the meat with a canvas to protect it from dew and rain. Never allow meat to become wet during the drying process.

Use salt, if it is available, in curing meat in damp, warm climates. This prevents spoiling and speeds up curing by drawing out moisture, although some elements of nutrition are lost. It also gives jerky a more agreeable taste for persons who are not accustomed to it.

Use the same amount of salt as in cooking meat — 1 teaspoonful to the pound. You can add 3 tablespoonfuls of pepper to each cup of salt, although it isn't really necessary. Some hunters also put in dry mustard and allspice to improve the flavor. When meat is sundried, pepper is often sprinkled over it to help ward off flies. Rub salt or mixed seasonings on the slices of meat, let them lie covered about 2 hours, then hang them up in the wind. When dripping or sweating stops, move them to the rack and kindle your fire.

Cured meat should be stored in waterproof bags or tight cans to protect it from moisture and mold. Indians and old-time plainsmen often pounded the hard chunks of jerky into a sort of fibrous meal and added fat, sugar, and wild berries to produce pemmican. Either the plain dried meat or the pemmican mixture can be eaten raw — or it can be softened with water, mixed with flour or cornmeal, and fried like sausage. You can also cook it with potatoes and onions, scramble it with eggs, or make it into gravy soup, or stew. Pounding the hard pieces with the ax head will reduce them to convenient size for cooking.

While more deer meat probably is jerked than any other kind, the lean parts of all big-game animals as well as beef and the breasts of gamebirds can be preserved by this method.

Big-game hides have a practical and monetary value even if you don't want to use them as trophies, so take a little care to prevent them from heating and softening, or shedding hair. A hide taken in cold weather need only be rough-scraped and dried in camp. Rough-scraping means to lay the skin over a smooth surface and then scrape or cut away fat, membrane, and meat sticking to it. Cut off tag ends and very bloody edges, pull the wrinkles out, and hang over a rope or pole in a shady place, hair side in. When almost dry, roll loosely with flesh side out. That way it should come through the home trip well.

In warm, humid weather you should scrape the hide more carefully and then apply salt to its flesh side. Remove all the debris, then spread the hide flat on the ground, hair side down, and rub salt into every square inch of surface. Salt absorbs moisture, thus hastening the drying process. It also tightens hair and prevents rotting. Even if hair is to be removed later in making buck-skin or leather, use salt now to give the hide better quality. When the salt covering the hide is soaking wet, scrape it off and put on a fresh, dry coating. When it's almost *but not quite* dry roll it loosely for transportation home. Rolling a very dry hide may cause unsightly crack lines that will show up after the skin has been tanned. It will be too late then to do much if anything to fix the damage. For best results, handle hides carefully.

CHAPTER XXIII

Don't Get Lost

A veteran woodsman tells how to find
your way through the wilderness

BY MAURICE H. DECKER

I WAS never lost in the woods in my life, Daniel Boone used to say. "But once I was mighty confused for three days."

Getting "confused" is a thing that could happen to any of us, particularly the man who hunts in remote, sparsely settled country. Guides of the northern woods know it, and they take pains to see that their clients don't go straying off, particularly those who display little woodsmanship.

Actually, most people become lost because of their own carelessness or lack of foresight. There are only a few things you can do when you are lost, but there's a lot you can do to prevent such a mishap. None of the precautions is a chore or a burden; in fact, some of them — map reading, for instance — can be fun. And when you go out you'll have a new measure of self-confidence.

First off, before you travel alone in an unfamiliar area, you should get a topographic map of it and become at least generally acquainted with its features. Topographic maps show the terrain in detail: trails, roads, streams, lakes, hills, mountains, etc. These maps are fascinating things to study, and a few hours with one will give you a pretty clear idea of an area.

Always carry a reliable compass and know how to use it. Few

people can depend alone on a sense of orientation. A man may think he's traveling in a straight course, for instance, when actually he's moving in a big circle. Detours around obstacles may throw him off course, too. He can't depend entirely on the position of the sun, for that changes. But if he carries a compass he'll always be pretty sure of his general course.

But when you add a compass to your hunting outfit, be sure to keep in mind two vital points. First, a compass will distinguish one direction from another, but it won't by itself tell you which of them is the right one to follow to reach a given goal. Second, the compass differs from other useful articles like your knife and waterproof matchbox. Those you can leave in a pocket until they're actually needed — but don't try that with a compass. If you leave it unconsulted and unread until you're confused about direction and don't know which way to go, chances are it won't help much.

The secret of finding your way through wilderness country with a compass — to be able to start out from camp and always find your way back — is simply to know your approximate position at all times in relation to the goal. Without this knowledge, the most expensive and highly specialized compass won't be worth a cent.

To know your position at all times with respect to some definite landmark when following unfamiliar trails is not so very difficult, but you must give constant attention and observation to the job. Pathfinding is three-fourths observation and only one-fourth compass reading.

Sometimes you can locate your position with compass bearings taken on several landmarks visible from a distance and recognizable on your map. More often, however, you obtain it by continual observation. Expert woodsmen do this more or less automatically as they walk because they have trained their eyes and brains by much practice.

The woodsman knows in which direction he is traveling and how far he goes. He balances the angles and distances of the legs of any irregular course against one another, and with a sort of constant dead reckoning always knows his position with respect to his starting point or his destination. You should do the same whenever there's some chance of becoming lost and then needing a compass reading to help you back home.

Here is how you do it: When you leave camp on a trail into unfamiliar territory, note the direction you travel. And don't trust to a check on the sun or wind or other natural signs. You should use your compass. That's what you pack it for, and its reading is easier to interpret and more trustworthy. When you cross a stream, consult the compass again and note which way the water flows and in which direction you move when you leave its bank. Repeat this when you pass outstanding landmarks and when you make any abrupt or angling turn off your original course.

This may be all you need to do on short, easy trips that do not carry you too far afield. If you started off toward the east, for instance, and later made some slight turns to the north, you realize you have to travel approximately southwest when you return. Knowing the direction, you check for it with the compass and follow the reading home.

An added precaution is necessary however, when you make longer trips in totally unknown country or are forced to detour around large obstacles such as lakes, swamps, or mountains. Now merely checking direction is not enough; you should also note the distance you travel on each leg or turn of the irregular course. This is very important in detouring, because when you walk half a mile south to miss some barrier, you have to walk the same distance north to get back on your original course.

Distance can be measured by counting paces or by checking the time with your watch. The latter method probably is most accurate, because it is quite easy to lose track of 10 or 100 paces when counting. The ordinary woods gait over fairly smooth terrain runs about 2½ miles an hour, but when the going is rougher this may drop to 2 miles. Time intervals can be translated into miles or yards if you wish, but this isn't necessary; if you walk a given distance in a quarter of an hour, you can do it again on your way back.

There are two ways to keep track of changes in course — in your mind and on paper. The trained woodsman usually relies on a mental map of his progress. This ability to remember the way has prompted people to credit him with a natural "homing" or direction-finding instinct, whereas actually a keen observation and good memory explain the gift.

The less experienced hunter may be able to get by in partly unfamiliar country with similar mental dead reckoning, but in a real wilderness he'll run fewer risks of becoming lost if he uses pencil and paper. With these he can plot his trail as he goes, jotting down the main directions taken and the approximate distances traveled. The data can be entered in a notebook or on ruled graph paper. (The ruling helps you keep the chart in true proportion and to scale). Or, you can trace your route over a regular printed map, preferably one of the topographical kind. When you don't use a map, it helps to lay out your path as a line on the plain paper, with bearings and distances written in at each change in course.

Plotting a trail on paper is especially useful in thick woods. Here everything looks about the same, you may have frequent detours, and you seldom have a chance to see far enough ahead to regulate your course by a distant landmark. When people become badly lost and travel in a circle, the locale usually is dense woods.

An important use of the compass is to make a rough map of the country surrounding your camp, to help you in any future emergency. It need not be more than a simple sketch that shows three or four conspicuous details. Even a mental picture of the district, including hills, mountains, rivers, and lakes, will help if you ever feel uncertain about which way to go back. When rivers are involved, always note or remember which way the water flows.

To map the physical features of the country surrounding the hunting camp can prevent serious accidents, because hunters easily lose their sense of direction while stalking game or tracking down wounded animals.

To start your map, put an X in the center of the paper to represent the campsite. If it is located on a river, lake shore, railroad, road, or telegraph line, plot in the main curves of such a base line so you will know which way to turn when you reach it. Also, in heading toward this base line on your way back to camp, you can employ the airlane pilot's method of finding a given point on a coastline. Instead of trying to hit this point exactly, he purposely bears to one side, the left for example. Then, when he reaches the coast, he merely bears right along it until he runs into the goal. If he had aimed directly for the point and missed it, he wouldn't have known which way to turn.

With your camp and its base line (if any) properly marked, look toward the horizon in all directions for conspicuous, easily identified landmarks. When you see one (it may be necessary to climb a tree for good visibility in timber), take a bearing on it with the compass and note the direction and the approximate distance away.

You can easily see the advantage of charting as many landmarks in as many different directions as possible. When you become lost all you have to do is walk to the nearest point marked on your map and then walk from it home. The map shows in which direction your camp lies, and your compass indicates the way exactly.

Your compass will also help you locate the site of your camp on a regular printed map. Take bearings on two or more landmarks visible from camp, which show up on the map. Draw lines along the bearings, and where these lines intersect will be the place where you stand. Again the topographical kind of map is best because it is made on a large scale and has contour lines to indicate and measure elevations, in addition to the more common features like rivers and lakes.

When working with printed maps, it is often necessary to allow for compass variation because the compass needle points to the magnetic pole and in many regions this direction differs widely from true north. The amount of variation for any certain place is usually noted in degrees on the margin of a printed map. If the variation is east you add this figure to your compass bearing; if west you subtract it to get the true direction.

Some compass models can be easily adjusted for variation, which considerably simplifies the job of pathfinding. In such cases follow the directions that accompany the instrument. Observe them too in other phases of route finding and map plotting, because all compasses are not alike. Some models for instance, have the letters standing for east and west reversed so the instrument can be pointed at an object and the bearing read from the needle.

After determining your course toward any given point, you must be careful to walk in as straight a line as possible. Sight over the compass toward some easily recognized object — a tree is very good — and then walk to it. Then take a new bearing on another point that lies in the same direction. You can also walk in a straight line by keeping two objects along your course in line with each other. Before you reach the first, pick another ahead. By repeating this process, you can lay off a straight course of considerable length.

If your hunting trips are short ones and in country partly familiar, a pocket compass that shows merely the main directions may serve you well. But for actual pathfinding and map making in wilderness country you will work better and more easily with a larger compass, one whose dial is at least 1 1/2 in. across and is graduated in degrees.

Graduation in degrees is important because you will take very few bearings that fall exactly on the principal compass "points." In most cases they must be identified and recorded in degrees. Most large compasses also carry sighting devices which help you lay off and follow accurate courses and some are mounted on transparent bases that hide less of the map when in use. These bases, too, are scored with metric and inch tables to help you plot courses and measure distances.

You can get broad-dial models with either dry or liquid-filled needle housings. The former are slower in use because their needles swing widely back and forth for some time before they come to rest and any slight jar is likely to start them moving again. However this swinging can be checked to some extent if you work the manual brake that keeps the needle locked when the compass is not being used. All dry-housing instruments need such a brake, for without it the needle bearing would speedily wear loose and lose accuracy.

Liquid-filled compasses also carry a dampening device and can be sighted over and checked for direction almost immediately. There was some trouble with war-surplus liquid models leaking, but regular production seems to be quite free of this fault. The liquid contains an antifreeze so the compass will operate in temperatures as low as 40 degrees below zero F.

An advantage of the liquid-dial model is that you need not always place it on top of a stump or level rock to take a bearing. In many instances sufficient accuracy is possible by simply holding the compass in your hand. The dial of any model, however, should be held level to keep the needle from binding.

Be sure no metal object lies close enough to your compass to deflect the needle when you consult it. An automobile, gun, knife, ax. or even a belt buckle may do this.

A compass will go wrong occasionally, but in most instances it is safer to trust its reading than your own mental notion about direction. Before you start a long trip have your compass checked for accuracy. You may only have to compare it with some known directions at home, or you can check it with a surveyor's transit.

If, however, you haven't used your compass and become lost on a hunting trip, you must figure out what to do to get out of your predicament.

The first rule is, stay calm. Panic is the worst possible thing that can happen to you, short of a disabling accident. It may, as a matter of fact, cause you to injure yourself or become even more hopelessly lost. Panic-stricken persons have dashed madly through the woods until completely exhausted, then succumbed to exposure. Keep your head, because a lost man is rarely as badly off as he thinks. Sit down and smoke. Take a drink of water, or eat a candy bar or sandwich. And reason things out.

What you must do next depends on your circumstances. If you have companions back at camp you'll be missed at mealtime. Eventually a search party will be sent out for you. Meantime you may have to spend a night in the woods, so prepare yourself for it by setting up some sort of brush shelter and gathering firewood. Assemble plenty, for your fire is going to serve as a signal to searchers, as well as a comfort to you. You'll want to keep it blazing all night long. If you think you'll be missed before dark, get green wood and brush that will send up a heavy column of smoke. If it doesn't attract searchers it may alarm a forest ranger, who'll come to see if he has a woods fire on his hands.

If you've been on your own, though, and know you won't be missed for a considerable time, you'll have to find your own way out. In that case, your next move will depend on the time of day. If there is still plenty of travel time left before nightfall you can utilize it. But first try to orientate yourself. Climb a tree or hill and look for some familiar landmark — a mountain, lake, or river, for instance — that will give you a key to your position.

If the afternoon is well along, with sunset near, stay where you are till morning. Struggling through the dark is risky and usually unproductive. You can't follow an accurate course, nor will you be able to see landmarks you passed on your outward journey. And you may hurt yourself.

Fortunately, most woodsmen are able to work out a solution as soon as they get their faculties working. Memory plays a great part in getting a lost hunter back on the right trail. But first he must make a start, and that involves a knowledge of the compass points. Even if he doesn't carry a compass there are ways of determining north and the other compass points.

For one thing, you know that the sun sets approximately in the west. You can determine the direction of its travel by watching the shadow cast by a tree. The shadow will move toward the east, the sun toward the west. Knowing that, you can determine north and south.

Even when the sun is hidden by clouds you can still make a directional check. Hold a slender object — a pin, match, straw, knife blade, etc. — upright on a polished surface, say your watchcase or thumbnail. Examine that surface until you see a faint shadow cast by the obscured sun. This trick works even when the sky is discouragingly overcast.

Knowing the position of the sun, you can use your watch as a compass. Aim the hour hand directly toward the sun. Now a point halfway between that hand and the figure 12 (the shortest way) marks south.

You can determine north after dark by the North Star, Polaris. First locate the Big Dipper, that familiar constellation of seven stars that actually looks like a dipper. The two stars that form the outer edge of the Big Dipper's bowl point to the North Star. (Practice finding Polaris during evenings at home; some day it may prove to be a good friend.)

When you have located Polaris, drive a couple of sticks into the ground to line up with it and point to it. Next morning they'll quickly tell you which way is north.

Now, we'll assume that you must find your own way out; know at least the general direction you took from camp (say, northeast); and are familiar with the compass bearings. You start back on a general course toward camp, using your eyesight and your memory. Concentrate on the back trail and try to recall as many details about it as possible: the different turns and detours, the landmarks and physical formations you passed. Don't overlook even the trivial things, for they may remind you of something important.

But don't forget, in making your way along a back trail, that you are looking at your surroundings from an entirely different angle, which makes them seem unfamiliar. It will be worth your while to pause, every little while, and look back along the trail you have just traveled to see if there are any familiar features you may have over-looked.

If you have no notion at all in which direction camp lies, or if you can't find your back trail, then you must do the next best thing: Find a safe way of getting *somewhere*. Unless you're lost in the remote wilds, you can walk in any direction and eventually run into some trace of civilization.

A stream or river will generally lead you to a farm or settlement, if there are any such in the region. Usually it's better not to try to walk along the banks, which may be brush grown or broken by feeder streams that will block you. Walk parallel to the stream at some distance, preferably along a ridge that will give you a good view of its twistings and turnings.

In mountain country you can follow a valley. If your course was uphill before you became lost, try to get back to lower ground. If you come across a dim trail or old road, remember that it may have been abandoned and lead nowhere. A road with signs of recent traffic is, of course, another thing.

To make sure you walk in a fairly straight line, not circling back to your starting point, sight the course ahead of you continuously. Do this by lining up two objects — trees, say — and keep them aligned as you walk. When you approach the first one, find another tree to line up with the second, and continue on in that fashion.

Halt occasionally and listen for sounds that indicate civilization — an ax blow, a train whistle, a rooster's crow. At intervals climb a tree and search for smoke. As you walk, shout or fire your rifle; three shots is a signal of distress. Listen for answering shots or shouts.

Becoming lost can be a minor incident or one that will spoil your trip and that of your friends. At best, it's a nuisance to everyone concerned; at worst, it may mean tragedy. So take the few precautions I have outlined and stay found at all times.